Painting Your House

INSIDE AND OUT

Painting Your House

INSIDE AND OUT

THUNDER BAY
P·R·E·S·S

San Diego, California

Thunder Bay Press
An imprint of the Advantage Publishers Group
5880 Oberlin Drive, San Diego, CA 92121-4794
www.thunderbaybooks.com

All notations of errors or omissions should be addressed to Thunder Bay Press, Editorial Department, at the above address. All other correspondence (author inquiries, permissions) concerning the content of this book should be addressed to Rockport Publishers, Inc., 33 Commercial Street, Gloucester, Massachusetts 01930-5089. Telephone: (978) 282-9590; Fax: (978) 283-2742; www.rockpub.com.

ISBN 1-59223-035-0

Library of Congress Cataloging-in-Publication Data available upon request.

Grateful acknowledgment is given to Judy Ostrow for her work from *Painting Rooms* on pages 10–143 and pages 298–301; to Francine Hornberger and Virginia Patterson for their work from *Painted Furniture* on pages 146–163; and to Bonnie Rosser Krims for her work from *The Perfectly Painted House* on pages 166–296.

Cover Images: Henry Wilson/The Interior Archive, top
　　　　　　　 Brian Vanden Brink, bottom

Printed in China

1 2 3 4 5 07 06 05 04 03

Contents

PAINTING
INSIDE

The Power of Paint

FOR THE COST OF SEVERAL CANS OF COLOR AND A FEW SIMPLE TOOLS, YOU HAVE THE POWER

TO TRANSFORM AN ORDINARY ROOM INTO SOMETHING MEMORABLE, BEAUTIFUL, AND COMFORTABLE.

AVAILABLE IN AN ALMOST INFINITE RAINBOW OF COLORS, PAINT HAS BECOME THE MOST EASILY

OBTAINABLE, VERSATILE, AND ECONOMICAL DECORATING MEDIUM.

Paint accomplishes myriad decorating tasks. It creates a unifying backdrop to harmonize an

eclectic group of furnishings. It highlights a collection of prized possessions. It accentuates

beautiful architectural features, making it easier to notice their detail. It brightens dull

surroundings, or softens an austere setting. It can be manipulated to mimic many kinds of

luxury materials – marble, precious metal, or exotic wood. With so much talent, paint has

become an indispensable ingredient for home decoration. *Painting Rooms* is designed as a

guidebook for using painted surfaces as a key component for decorating interiors.

section one

Choosing and Using Paint covers painting materials—the products, tools, and techniques that produce a range of looks and styles that readers can choose to duplicate in their personal spaces:

- Choosing the Right Paint
- Smooth Coatings
- Broken Color Effects
- Tools of the Trade
- Paint Practice

section two

How to Get the Perfect Color will demystify and unstress the process of bringing color home. It makes the transition from learning about the product and its capabilities to picking paint colors and effects that will complete a successful decorating plan:

- Painting with Blue
- Painting with Red
- Painting with Yellow
- Painting with Green
- Painting with Violet
- Painting with Orange
- Painting with Neutrals
- Change Color to Change the Mood

Often, when confronted with aisles of paint cans and thousands of color chips, we are seized by a kind of panic, a color identity crisis. We beat a retreat to white and beige—with so much choice, the potential for error seems great; color seems like a risky business.

To eliminate that sense of risk, the chapters in Section Two present images of finished rooms, grouped by color in the six hues of the spectrum, plus a section on neutrals—black, white, and brown. Selected not only for visual beauty, each photograph is also a hardworking tool to identify how paint color relates to its environment and acts with other furnishings to achieve beauty, harmony, and balance.

This section of the book follows no specific decorating dictum, no unbreakable rule. For, while such adages abound, the true test of a color and decorating plan is whether, finally, it is livable—and enjoyably so. We hope that *Painting Rooms* will help any reader learn many ways to live happily with color.

The Language of Color

- A *hue* is another name for a color.

- A *tint* is a color to which white has been added.

- A *tone* is a color to which gray has been added.

- A *shade* is a color to which black has been added.

- When talking about the *value* of a color, what is meant is its relative lightness or darkness compared to other colors. Think of a black-and-white photograph; colors of the same value will be perceived as the same shade of gray. To look at a room in terms of the values of its various colors, squint as you observe it. You will begin to see the values of objects in the room, and which are the same. Some objects fade into shadow (dark values) and some appear brighter than the others (light values).

- *Saturation* of a color relates to its darkness or density of color; a fully saturated color has a very dark, almost black, tone and will appear black or nearly so in a black-and-white photograph.

choosing the right paint

	WHAT IT DOES	WHAT IT'S GOOD FOR	THINGS TO CONSIDER
WATER-BASED PAINT: **Latex**	Spreads easily; cleans up with soap and water	All interior applications; may be diluted with water for broken color effects	Inexpensive brands may lack durability
Acrylic	Same as latex; higher quality solids	All interior applications; as above	Best quality are 100% acrylic
OIL-BASED PAINT:	Spreads evenly; durable finish; longer drying time than water-based products	All interior applications; dilute with its solvent (usually mineral spirits) for broken color application	Must be cleaned with mineral spirits or other solvents; produces fumes; requires excellent ventilation during application and drying
SPECIALTY PAINTS: **Glazes**	Clear or translucent coating for broken color effects; may be oil- or water-based; should be applied over opaque base.	Can be easily manipulated for many special effects	Relatively short drying time requires quick application; working this paint with a partner is helpful
Milk paints	Vintage recipe for paint that provides eco-friendly finish; available as a powder to be mixed with water	Provides a smooth, dead-flat finish; good for walls and furniture in colonial or other vintage rooms	Somewhat soft finish needs to be protected with clear polyurethane or wax; surfaces other than raw wood should be primed
Ecofriendly Paints	Few or no VOCs; many brands also formulated without harmful chemicals	Among the brands are products for most interior applications	Because many pigments contain VOCs, some brands only available in lighter colors

WHAT IT DOES	WHAT IT'S GOOD FOR	THINGS TO CONSIDER

Artists' Acrylics

Fine arts paints, water-based; intensely pigmented	Good for broken color effects when small amounts of a color are needed	Intense colors mean these paints need to be diluted for lighter tints

Universal tints

Not a paint; these are pigments used for adding color	Good for adjusting to a specific custom color	Pigments are quite intense; should be added to paint drop by drop

Metallic pigments

Available as powder; mix with other paints	Add the sheen of various metals to a paint medium	Handle carefully; wear mask and gloves

Crackling Medium

Clear product applied over a base coat, then overpainted with a second opaque layer; this product makes the second layer crack to an antiqued, alligatored finish	For creating an aged, distressed appearance on woodwork, furniture, and walls	Best for use with decorative trim, paneling, doors, or cabinet surfaces; more difficult to get great results on large expanses of wall

Textured paints

Usually acrylics; mixed with a textured medium – small acrylic beads or sand – to produce a visibly textured finish	Produces a look that imitates suede or other textured material	Difficult to remove; application usually requires more paint than ordinary opaque coatings

Primers

Creates a smooth surface to which new layers of paint can adhere	Needed when changing colors, especially dark to light, to prevent bleed-through; provides surface integrity for any paint job	Match primers and paints from same manufacturer; ask for advice when painting special surfaces: glass, metal, plastic, etc. These may require special primers

getting the effects you want

SMOOTH COATINGS:	WHAT IT DOES	WHAT IT'S GOOD FOR	THINGS TO CONSIDER
Flat finish	Provides a velvet smooth, non-reflective coating; hides wall defects	Authentic finish for vintage colonial style rooms; good background for art	Difficult to clean; sponge marks and fingerprints may show; use in low-traffic areas
Eggshell	Minimally reflective surface; acceptable base coat for broken color finishes	Same applications as flat finish	Easier to clean than flat finishes
Satin or Pearl	Slightly reflective; often chosen for trim, moldings in flat-finished rooms; excellent base for broken color finishes	Trim or walls where easy cleaning and low shine are important	Easy to clean; smooth surface may reveal wall flaws; requires good wall prep
Semigloss	Durable, somewhat glossy finish; good for trim, doors, molding	Good finish for high-traffic areas, as well as bathrooms and kitchens, where cleaning is an issue	Good wall preparation is key; walls must be clean and smooth for best results
High-gloss	Very glossy and durable finish	Same applications as semi-gloss; use where high shine is desirable	Glossy paint shows every wall flaw; smooth wall essential for best results
Textured finishes	Depending on degree of texture, gives impression of suede, sand, or nubby fabric	Use where texture makes sense; for the look of aged or rough walls, or to duplicate textured fabric	Requires more paint than other smooth coatings for effective coverage; once applied, can be difficult and messy to remove

WHAT IT DOES	WHAT IT'S GOOD FOR	THINGS TO CONSIDER	BROKEN COLOR EFFECTS:
			Colorwashing
Gives appearance of light texture; easy to apply	A method to apply color at less-than-full intensity for a softer look in rooms	For a uniform look, use consistent stroke; for freer looks, vary the stroking technique	
			Stippling
Provides a light, dappled appearance	Delicate and elegant effect for translucent color, for whole rooms or room features such as molding and trim	Somewhat difficult; execute this effect with a partner	
			Sponging
Easy effect for applying multiple layers of translucent color	Whole room treatments anywhere in the home; or use as accent treatment on a single wall or feature	Easiest of the broken color finishes; for most delicate looks, must use fine, evenly pored sponges	
			Ragging On
Provides an appealing, random texture	Lovely look for walls in formal rooms	Fairly easy; needs a light touch in applying	
			Ragging Off
Provides a beautiful, complex, and delicate texture	As above	Somewhat difficult; execute this effect with a partner	

getting the effects you want

	WHAT IT DOES	WHAT IT'S GOOD FOR	THINGS TO CONSIDER
BROKEN COLOR EFFECTS:			
Dragging	Striated effect; looks rich and elegant	Use for cabinets, molding, wainscoting. Straight lines difficult to apply on full length walls	Not too difficult when working small areas
Combing Techniques	Like dragging, combing provides a striated effect that can be worked in many patterns	A great look for informal rooms and country houses	As above; take care to keep combing tool clean between strokes, so pattern stays clear
Stenciling	Easy way to apply a repeat pattern to walls	Use anywhere; great as a border device, or as an allover pattern—like wallpaper	Very easy
Reverse Stenciling	Requires multiple templates of same design	Can provide very subtle patterning when colors close in tone are used	Easy

WHAT IT DOES	WHAT IT'S GOOD FOR	THINGS TO CONSIDER
Provides the look of aged or distressed painted wood	Excellent for an antique look for small areas; doors, trim, cabinetry	Somewhat difficult as a total wall treatment; crackling will always create a random, not a uniform pattern
The look of marble for the price of two or three cans of paint	Use anywhere marble is used; mantels, trim and woodwork, tabletops, etc. Whole marble walls are *only* for very luxurious environments	Somewhat difficult but a great deal of fun; practicing this technique is essential
Provides a softly aged look	Good for walls or details in period homes	Fairly easy technique
Very beautiful and elegant wall finish	Superb for formal rooms	Somewhat difficult; technique requires lots of energy
Absolutely fabulous look of lace	Walls are difficult and the materials cost is somewhat high; use this technique for simpler projects – drawer fronts, tabletops	A great deal of work and quite expensive; must work with a partner for walls, and the results will be worth the effort

BROKEN COLOR EFFECTS:

Crackling

Marbling

Antiquing

Parchment

Lace

CHOOSING AND USING PAINT

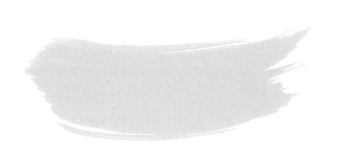

Welcome to the virtual paint aisle: In this section you can explore the different kinds of paint products – oil-based, water-based, specialty paints – their characteristics, and the types of projects best suited to their attributes.

Choosing the Right Paint

TODAY'S PAINT STORES OFFER SUCH A WIDE SELECTION OF PRODUCTS THAT COLOR BECOMES JUST

ONE OF THE MAJOR DECISIONS TO BE MADE WHEN EMBARKING ON A PAINTING PROJECT. EVEN

AFTER SELECTING THE TECHNIQUE—EITHER A SMOOTH OR A MANIPULATED FINAL FINISH—YOU

MUST CHOOSE THE RIGHT PRODUCTS FOR EVERY LAYER.

The first choice is the carrier, or liquid base, of a paint product. Modern paints offer two choices

for that portion of paint that makes it spreadable—oil or water. In general, whichever carrier is

used for the first coat of paint will determine any and all layers that are applied on top of it.

Water-base over water-base, oil-base over oil-base is the general rule, with few exceptions.

While almost infinite choice of color, texture, and overall effect of the final result is available

from either oil- or water-based paint media, each has characteristics of application, drying time,

ease of use, and environmental consequences that make this basic choice an important one.

In addition to the conventional choice between water-based latex and acrylic paints, and oil-

based paints, there are other options in water-based products to meet environmental concerns

or achieve a special decorative look. These are described later in the chapter.

water-based paints

○ **LATEX**

Years ago, latex referred to a natural plant extract. It is now used to describe any of a number of mainly synthetic resins that maintain flexibility over time. The binders, which hold a latex, water-based paint to the painting surface, are made up of these synthetic resins, usually polyvinyl acetate, acrylic resins, or a combination of the two.

○ **PURE ACRYLIC**

Pure acrylic paints are usually of higher quality and more expensive than other latex paints. The paint label will generally list ingredients, so read the label before buying.

○ **LATEX ADVANTAGES:**

Constant improvements in paint technology have made water-based latex products the top-sellers in the paint aisle. They are easy to apply, and though they dry quickly, newer formulations eliminate brush marks in the glossier sheens, a problem with early latex paint. Many of these products have very little paint odor, and all clean up with soap and water, making them even more user-friendly.

○ **LATEX DISADVANTAGES:**

On the downside, decorative painters warn that the quick drying time of latex products can wreak havoc with a broken color finish, since these paints may dry before a mistake can be corrected. However, there are several ways to diminish this disadvantage, covered later in this chapter.

oil-based paints

Oil-based paints have traditionally used a drying oil as their binder—the part that holds paint on a surface. While linseed, tung, or soy oils were the binders in early oil-based interior and exterior paints, these have been replaced in modern times with oils modified into a synthetic polymer, called an alkyd.

○ **ALKYDS**

The alkyd resin is then dissolved into a petroleum-based solvent such as mineral spirits, which forms the liquid carrier of the oil-based paint. Thus alkyd has become a term that is generally synonymous with oil-based paint.

○ **OIL-BASE ADVANTAGES:**

Oil-based paints have a long history of use by professional painters because of how smoothly they coat a surface and how long the finish endures. Their extended drying time allows brush marks to smooth out while the paint dries, and oil-based products cure to a desirably durable finish. When using oil-based products for manipulated, broken color finishes, the longer drying time (also known as "open" time) allows the decorative painter to correct mistakes before they dry, making the final finish less prone to flaws.

▫ OIL-BASED DISADVANTAGES:

While it is true that an oil-based finish makes a great looking wall covering, there are certain drawbacks to consider. Cleanup can be complex and messy, as equipment and spills must be cleaned with the appropriate solvent, usually mineral spirits or turpentine, both toxic (follow directions on the paint label regarding the appropriate cleaner.) Oil-based paints, made with petroleum-based solvent, have a long-lasting, sometimes noxious odor that requires excellent ventilation in any room where the paint is applied, until it dries. Prolonged exposure to these fumes is not advisable. Thus, children and pets (and you) will not be able to comfortably use a room while it is being primed, painted and/or decorated with a broken color finish executed in oil-based paints.

Second, the carrier in oil-based paint (petroleum-based solvent) is a volatile organic compound (VOC), which not only creates odors but also contributes to poor air quality indoors and outdoors. VOCs react with other pollutants to create ozone, contributing to a range of problems, including global warming.

▫ OIL-BASED VS. LATEX

While these concerns may make the choice clear, bear in mind that a premium quality oil-base paint will not have to be applied as frequently as, for example, a bargain brand of latex paint. The premium oil finish may look beautiful for a decade or more, while the inexpensive latex brand keeps its good looks for three years or less. Water-based latex and acrylic paints contribute VOCs to the environment, though not in as great a quantity as oil paints, and using them every couple of years can add nearly as much ozone to the atmosphere as the once-a-decade application of oil finish. So, factor in the longevity of a paint finish in the final equation and decision.

other interior paints

Opaque oil-based and water-based latex and acrylic paints together represent a very high percentage of the paint market. Nonetheless, there remain many other types of coating with decorative interior applications. Some special effects require transparent glazing liquids, powdered pigments, and other less common materials; other products offer the consumer the opportunity to choose paint with very low toxicity and other ecofriendly attributes. Following is a roundup of these other varieties of paint.

□ **GLAZES**
Liquid glazes, which come in all sheen levels and have a slippery texture, form the basic application medium for manipulated finishes. Glazes can be transparent, pre-tinted with pigments, or mixed by the decorative painter with paints or pigment powders. They can provide depth and luminosity to walls, as well as the decorative enhancement of applied effects. This decorative medium has become so popular that nearly every major paint manufacturer now offers a line of clear and colored glazes.

□ **OIL-BASED GLAZES**
Oil-based glazes can be used with walls and surfaces base-coated with oil paint.

□ **WATER-BASED GLAZES**
Water-based glazes are applied over water-based paint.

□ **GLAZE TIPS**
Glazes differ from paint in that their drying time is quite short; when using them for walls, working quickly becomes an important part of the process, as unblended glaze on a wall can create unsightly lines in a painted effect. Decorative painters recommend that do-it-yourselfers work in tandem with a helper; one to apply glaze, one to work the effect. A bit of practice on a large piece of board can help perfect technique before the glaze is applied to large areas of wall. Some paint experts recommend using an extender product in the glaze to lengthen its "open" (drying) time.

□ **MILK PAINT**
An age-old finish used by rural folk to add color to walls and furnishings, milk paint has enjoyed a recent comeback.

□ **MILK PAINT: BASICS**
While the recipes may vary among milk paint manufacturers, the basic ingredients are casein (milk protein), lime, clay, and natural earth pigments. The paint is sold as a powder (once moistened with its carrier—ordinary water—it must be used quickly or the paint will sour).

□ **MILK PAINT: FINISH**
Milk paint provides a warm, dead-flat finish with a slightly grainy appearance. Milk paint is an excellent choice for coating bare wood, as it needs no primer. On surfaces that have been previously finished, an acrylic additive can be mixed with the first coat; consult the manufacturer for additional advice on surface preparation.

□ **MILK PAINT DISADVANTAGES:**
Milk paint does have one drawback; this natural, environmentally friendly product has no sealing qualities and is thus susceptible to water spotting and staining. It can be sealed with a coat of beeswax for an equally earth-friendly layer of protection, and many people with vintage homes or decor like the aged, distressed look of a worn finish. However, to preserve an unblemished appearance, the best protection is a topcoat of flat, clear acrylic finish.

ECOFRIENDLY PAINTS

Today, water-based paints are formulated with fewer volatile organic compounds (VOCs) than ever before; major manufacturers have also developed low- or no-VOC lines, driven by demand from health care facilities for paints that would not disrupt human traffic and habitation while they are being applied. Many small companies make paints with no or low VOCs, and they add to this feature a commitment to low or very minimally toxic ingredients. For those concerned about the environment, and people with special health concerns, these ecofriendly paints are worth investigating. Ask your paint dealer about major manufacturers' lines of low-VOC products; a listing of producers of ecofriendly paints can be found in the Resources section.

PAINT BOX

Getting a Consistent Metallic Look

SOME MANUFACTURERS NOW OFFER WALL PAINT WITH A LUMINOUS, METALLIC LOOK, ALTHOUGH MANY DO-IT-YOURSELFERS FIND IT DIFFICULT TO GET A PERFECT, SHIMMERING FINISH WITH THESE READY-MADE PAINTS.

TO IMPROVE SMOOTH COVERAGE AND FINISH MIX THE METALLIC PAINT WITH AN EQUAL QUANTITY OF OPAQUE PAINT IN A RELATED COLOR (GRAY WITH SILVER METALLIC, YELLOW WITH GOLD FINISHES).

ECOFRIENDLY: COLOR RANGE

Note, however, that since VOCs can be found in many commonly used colorants, many low-VOC paints from major producers are available only in light colors. The color ranges for each company differ, so request color charts and other information when consulting a local dealer or contacting these manufacturers.

ARTISTS' ACRYLICS

Sometimes only a small amount of a color is needed for a detail or decorative feature in a painting project, and less than a quart or pint of water-based paint is needed. Quarts are usually the smallest size available for major manufacturers' custom colors; stock colors are usually offered in pints. In this case, buy a tube of artists' acrylic paint. Since the paint colors are very intense, the color may be tinted with white, darkened with black, or toned down with a dab of its complement.

UNIVERSAL TINTS

These are the components used in the paint store to mix custom colors. Available in small bottles, the consumer may buy them for do-it-yourself tinting of paint. Keep in mind that universal tints cannot be used on their own (they are pigments, not paint); universal tints are also quite intense, so coloring your own paint should be a careful process, tinting drop by drop until the right color is achieved. Universal colorants can be used to tint both oil- and water-based paints.

METALLIC PIGMENTS

Metallic finishes can add drama or detail to a painted room. Create a metallic finish by mixing metallic powders — available for all the looks of metal, from chrome to gold — in the wall paint or glaze. The powders should be handled carefully; wear disposable gloves and a mask to protect skin and prevent inhalation of the powders; they are toxic.

☐ **CRACKLING MEDIUM**

This water-based product creates an interesting, aged look when it is brushed on between two layers of paint or glaze, causing the top coat to crack and reveal the base coat. Do not use oil-based paint over this water-based medium.

primers

With few exceptions, walls and other surfaces require a coat of primer to promote a clean, smooth finish when the paint is applied. Use the manufacturer's recommended primer product for the best results. When painting in deep colors, a tinted primer coat is often recommended, though opinions vary as to whether this will affect the color of the final paint coating (some pros insist that a color primer will save additional coats of paint and not affect final appearance; others disagree.) For special surfaces—metal, plastic, painting over wallpaper, painting previously stained or waxed surfaces—your paint dealer can recommend an appropriate product.

paint quality

Not all paints are created equal; the quality of the final finish depends not only on the painter's skill, but also on the good chemistry and integrity of the coating. Browsing the paint store, it becomes apparent that paint is available at many price points, costing as little as ten dollars a gallon and as much as one hundred dollars. What is the meaning of such a discrepancy?

☐ **PIGMENTS AND COVERAGE**

Quality ingredients are expensive, and the most expensive of these are the pigments used in paint formulation. Titanium dioxide is the portion of paint pigmentation that provides hiding power, and it is a costly substance. Good colorants also add to the price. Substituting inexpensive fillers for these ingredients brings down the cost of a can of paint, but the results can be disappointing, and worse, short-lived on the wall.

☐ **PREMIUM PAINTS**

In the realm of super-premium paints (fifty dollars and more per gallon), complex approaches to color that use five, eight, or a dozen different pigments to create beautiful and luminous paint hues make up a big percentage of the purchase price. Full-spectrum coloring, as it is called, combined with the highest quality binders and, in the case of oil-based paints, superior grades of solvent, provide beautiful finished surfaces that will last far longer than ordinary bargain or mid-grade paints.

Of course, quick and inexpensive may be the road you finally choose. But consider that your time and effort are valuable commodities; for the best, longest-lasting results, use the finest paint your budget can manage.

Smooth Coatings

THE CLEAN LOOK OF A SMOOTH, UNBROKEN WALL FINISH HAS LONG BEEN THE MOST POPULAR

PAINT APPLICATION FOR INTERIORS. EVEN IF THE ROOM WILL BE DECORATED WITH ADDITIONAL

LAYERS OF MANIPULATED PAINT, A SMOOTH BASE OF A SINGLE COLOR COMPOSES THE UNDERLYING

WALL TREATMENT FOR MOST SPECIAL EFFECTS. Whatever final result a do-it-yourselfer wishes to

achieve, it becomes necessary to master the art of choosing and applying a smooth coat of paint.

To help readers decide on just the right smooth coat, this chapter explores and explains the decorative benefits and the challenges of the many smooth looks of paint.

○ **SMOOTH COATINGS ADVANTAGES:**
Like a carpet, or coordinated window treatments, an unbroken expanse of colored wall becomes a distinctive feature that creates a mood, and at the same time functions as a unifying background for the furnishings and activity within a space. The right wall color can enliven and enhance a room's assets. A color that plays to a room's strengths, coordinating with its positive features – good light, spaciousness (or coziness), nice architectural detail – can positively affect the overall decorative impact and comfort level of a space.

○ **SMOOTH COATINGS DISADVANTAGES:**
Yet smooth coatings are demanding; with the exception of dead-flat paints, walls finished in layers of unbroken color must be thoroughly prepared, as any degree of gloss will reveal inherent flaws in the base surface. And, in spite of its effectiveness as a concealer, flat paint may be more difficult to clean and maintain than other coatings.

PAINT BOX

Base Coats for Broken Color Finishes

FLAT PAINTS ARE GOOD FOR MANY DECORATIVE APPLICATIONS, BUT DO NOT MAKE ACCEPTABLE BASE COATINGS FOR MANIPULATED LAYERS OF BROKEN COLOR FINISHES. WHEN APPLYING A **SMOOTH COATING AS A BASE COAT** FOR A MANIPULATED PAINT TECHNIQUE, USE A PAINT WITH SOME SHEEN. MANY DECORATIVE PAINTERS RECOMMEND SATIN (PEARL) AS AN UNDERCOAT.

---

what's in a paint?

All paints have three basic components.

- *Pigments* provide color and hiding power.
- *Binders* hold the pigment together, and provide the integrity and adhesion of the paint film.
- The *carrier* is the liquid that gives paint its consistency, so that pigment and binder can be applied to a surface.
- *Additives*. Many products also have additives, used to stabilize, thicken, defoam, or prevent the growth of bacteria in paint.

○ **SOLIDS AND SURFACE**
The pigment and binder are the components that remain on a surface when paint dries; together, they are the solids in paint.

○ **PIGMENT AND SHEEN**
Paint sheen – its degree of glossiness – is determined by the proportion of pigment to binder. High-gloss paints have a lower ratio of pigment to binder; matte finish paint has the highest proportion of pigment.

flat finish

Also called matte, flat paint has no shine and provides excellent coverage to most properly prepared surfaces. Because this coating does not reflect light, it conceals a multitude of flaws, so hairline cracks and dings seem to disappear. Many contractors like to paint new drywall with flat finish paint, since it does a good job of hiding taped drywall seams, and is easy to touch up.

FLAT FINISH: PAINT TYPES

Matte finish paints can be oil- or water-based, and their formulas and consistencies vary with the manufacturer. In addition to latex and acrylic water-based paints, milk paint and other ecofriendly formulas also have a flat finish.

FLAT FINISH: COVERAGE AND QUALITY

While every brand of flat-finish paint will provide a covering that looks smooth and hides wall defects, maintenance of these surfaces will vary according to each brand and its quality. Low-cost water-based paints do not clean up easily, often showing marks where a sponge has passed. The best quality, and thus the most expensive, flat-finish paints are the easiest to maintain.

FLAT FINISH: USES

Because of maintenance issues, use flat-finish paints in low-traffic areas less susceptible to staining and spotting; flats are also the generally preferred finish for ceilings. Traditionally used in galleries and on theatre backdrops, flat finishes are highly desirable for wall finishes that serve as background for displaying art, sculpture, and textiles. Interior designers sometimes specify flat finishes for a room that is "busy" with furnishings, patterns, and accessories; the matte walls create an almost velvety, fabric-like canvas for the room.

FLAT FINISH: ANTIQUE LOOKS

Matte-finished walls are also a natural treatment for antique homes, particularly old farmhouses and ancient cottages, which were originally decorated with flat-finish homemade paints made with earth pigments.

eggshell finish

Looking at paint chips finished with eggshell and matte paints side by side, it is often difficult to discern the difference. The very soft sheen of eggshell can usually be seen by holding the two chips at an angle and viewing them sideways, rather than straight on.

EGGSHELL FINISH: USES

The low reflectivity of eggshell finish makes it desirable for the same uses as matte finish, with the additional benefit of easier maintenance. Most eggshell finish paints can be washed more satisfactorily than dead-flat finishes.

EGGSHELL FINISH: WEAR AND TEAR

Nonetheless, this wall surface is still somewhat fragile; confine eggshell-finished surfaces to rooms where they will avoid constant wear and tear from errant fingerprints, moving furniture, and heavy traffic of people and pets. Because it does possess some very subtle sheen, eggshell can be used as a base coat for manipulated finishes.

satin finish

Satin finish paints have sufficient sheen to noticeably reflect the light in a room with a soft surface glow. Satin looks the way it sounds, a smooth covering for walls, like the gently shimmering fabric from which it gets its name.

SATIN FINISH: COVERAGE

Because of its sheen, walls finished with satin paints require more preparation than flat or eggshell-finished walls. Light will detect flaws with uncanny precision, so walls must be adequately prepared; dents and cracks should be repaired, and bumps and lumps should be sanded smooth.

SATIN FINISH: USES

Use a satin finish where increased light will enhance a space: in a dark hallway lit by wall sconces; in small rooms painted in deep colors, where lamplight can create a cozy feeling at night; in large, light spaces where the reflectivity will improve brightness, without glare. A satin finish provides the glow, without the shine.

SATIN FINISH: TRIM

Satin finish can be used as a coating for trim when the walls are painted in flat or eggshell finish; satin's slight sheen will look marginally brighter than the walls when used in this way, thus accentuating details of molding and other woodwork.

semigloss finish

Quick cleanups and durability make semi-gloss paints a popular choice for high-traffic and high-moisture areas. Available in oil- and water-based products, a semi-gloss sheen provides a distinctly smooth and reflective surface that is easy to maintain.

☐ **SEMIGLOSS FINISH: SURFACE**
Repaired, sanded, and cleaned surfaces create the base for a wall or trim treatment in semigloss paint, as shiny surfaces will accentuate flaws. While a finished semi-gloss treatment provides a delightfully glowing surface and easy maintenance, extra care in preparing the painting base will ensure a beautiful, long lasting paint job.

high-gloss finish

The hard, very shiny finish of high-gloss paints makes them an excellent choice wherever durability is a priority.

☐ **HIGH-GLOSS FINISH: USES**
Their high-polished look and easy main-tenance make glossy enamels appropriate for trim, doors, and cabinets, as all of these surfaces get handled more frequently than expanses of wall.

☐ **HIGH-GLOSS FINISH: SURFACE**
Applied to properly prepared, smooth walls, a coating of high-gloss paint has a glasslike surface. Use high-gloss products on walls in places where their reflective capability is desirable – dark rooms, windowless hallways, and closets.

☐ **HIGH-GLOSS FINISH: PAINT TYPES**
High-gloss products are available in oil- and water-based formulations. Because of the sometimes noxious fumes, compli-cated cleanup, and longer drying times of oil-based products, water-based gloss paints are often preferred for interior projects.

textured finishes

Paints premixed with ingredients that provide texture – sand, for example – are an easy way to create an interesting wall finish with a coating that is applied in the same manner as untextured smooth paints.

☐ **TEXTURED PAINT: SURFACE**
Textured paints usually require two coats for a smooth, seamless finish; for best results, closely follow manufacturers' instructions for application and drying time between coats. Properly applied, a textured paint will provide an interest-ing surface effect without manipulating the paint.

☐ **TEXTURED PAINT: COVERAGE**
Because of the extra bulk of textured paints, they will usually provide less coverage per gallon than nontextured products. Check the manufacturer's spread rate, which is listed on the con-tainer, to gauge how many square feet one gallon will cover, and figure paint needs accordingly.

PAINT BOX

Enamel Paints

ENAMEL USED TO MEAN OIL-BASED PAINTS WITH SHEEN. NOW, TO THE UNENDING CONFUSION OF CONSUMERS, THIS WORD **REFERS TO ANY PAINT WITH SHEEN,** WHETHER WATER- OR OIL-BASED. THUS ALL PAINTS WITH SHEEN, INCLUDING EGGSHELL, CAN BE IDENTIFIED AS ENAMELS.

A Sheen by Any Other Name...

WHILE FLAT, EGGSHELL, SATIN, SEMIGLOSS, AND HIGH-GLOSS ARE STANDARD NAMES **FOR THE VARYING SHEEN LEVELS OF PAINT,** SOME MANUFACTURERS OFFER INTERMEDIATE SHEENS, OR CALL THEIR PRODUCTS BY DIFFERENT NAMES. **GLOSS** CAN SOMETIMES MEAN A SHEEN LEVEL BETWEEN SEMIGLOSS AND HIGH-GLOSS.

PEARL CAN BE FOUND BETWEEN SATIN AND SEMIGLOSS; IN SOME CASES, IT IS THE NAME FOR THE WATER-BASED VERSION OF SATIN. ASK THE PAINT DEALER FOR A CARD OR CHIP SAMPLE THAT SHOWS PRODUCT SHEEN LEVELS FOR A PARTICULAR MANU-FACTURER BEFORE PURCHASING THE PAINT.

Broken Color Effects

THE TRANSFORMING POTENTIAL OF PAINT DOES NOT END WITH A CHOICE OF COLOR OR SHEEN.

BECAUSE OF ITS VISCOSITY, PAINT CAN EASILY BE MANIPULATED WITH A VARIETY OF TOOLS, FROM

CRUNCHED-UP PLASTIC BAGS TO GOOSE FEATHERS. Applied over a smooth base coat, these

manipulated layers are known as broken color effects. They offer the home painter the oppor-

tunity to add pattern, texture, and layers of color to the painted wall.

Like walls finished with wallpaper or fabric, walls treated with a broken color technique provide

an additional dimension to a scheme. Walls created with layers of *paint in motion* possess a

lively, vibrant quality that makes a powerful and memorable impression.

Some effects are quite easy for one person to apply and yield excellent results, even to beginners.

Other techniques need time and practice to master; the most complex ones require that two

people work together as a team.

Each technique in this chapter includes a general recipe, complete with a list of tools and

materials, as well as step-by-step instructions. Along with this technical guidance are some

ideas about the best uses for each method and helpful tips to make the process more effective

and successful.

colorwashing

An easy technique, colorwashing hides a multitude of sins; flaws in the base coat will disappear under the almost playful strokes with which the glaze is applied. Because the stroking technique is free, light, and somewhat random, use colorwashing in informal spaces – bedrooms, family rooms, and in homes decorated in a relaxed or rustic style. Aged plaster walls, or walls textured or distressed to achieve this effect, have an even more dramatic appearance when they are lightly colorwashed.

Practice this technique on a piece of board to discover the stroke and resulting effect that you find attractive and satisfying.

HOW TO COLORWASH

TOOLS:

- A wide (4" [10 cm]) brush for large expanses of wall
- A smaller (2" or 3" [5 cm or 8 cm]) brush for smaller spaces
- Small, clean paint can or coffee can

INGREDIENTS:

- A clean base coat in satin (pearl) or shinier
- Glaze for colorwashing (use oil- or water-based products; oil finishes will allow more time before the glaze dries.)

1. Tape off and/or mask any areas that will not be painted; apply the base coat with a roller. Allow the paint to dry thoroughly.
2. Thoroughly mix the glazing liquid; dip your brush in about a third of the way, knocking off any drips into the can.
3. Starting with an upper corner, work across and down the wall, applying the glaze in a dance-like movement of the brush. Use a crisscross, zigzag, or short, curvy stroke. Continue applying the glaze, redipping the brush as needed, until each wall is complete.

NOTE:

Glaze has a somewhat short working time; each manufacturer's product may be a little different. If the glaze has dried and there is a pronounced *stop point* or line in the colorwash application, you can paint over the mistake with the base color, allow it to dry, and colorwash again with the glaze.

stippling

Stippling glaze on a painted base creates an especially elegant effect; it looks wonderful applied to moldings, window trim, and cabinetry. This technique will subtly enhance either walls or trim in formal rooms full of luxurious fabrics and light-boned furnishings.

Stippling is a subtractive process; the glaze layer is stippled immediately after it is applied, which removes some of the glaze. Working quickly is a must for this technique, so work with a partner for best results. Using an oil-base coat and oil-glazing medium will give you more time to work.

HOW TO STIPPLE

TOOLS:

- A good stippling brush (use the largest brush you can comfortably handle, and invest in a brush of high quality. A large staining brush with lots of bouncy bristles can substitute, if a stippling tool cannot be found.)
- A small roller (4" [10 cm]) for applying glaze (use a roller sleeve with 1/2" [1 cm] nap)
- Rolling tray with disposable tray liner

INGREDIENTS:

- A clean base coat in satin (pearl) or shinier
- A glaze for stippling

You will need two people to complete this effect: one to roll the glaze on; one to stipple it off.

① Tape off and mask all areas adjacent to the surface being painted; apply the base coat with a roller; allow the paint to dry thoroughly.
② Work from top to bottom, and left to right; work quickly. The person applying glaze should load the small roller lightly, then roll it on from top to bottom; then the second person stipples the freshly rolled glaze.
③ To stipple, pounce the brush lightly – in a straight-on movement, not at an angle – against the glazed area, then remove the glaze taken up by the brush. (Either wear pants that you don't care about, or keep copious amounts of paper towels right next to you so that you can wipe off the stipple brush after each pounce.) The more you stipple an area, the more glaze will be removed, and the finer the finished effect will become.
④ Work with even pressure on the brush, at even speed. Complete a whole area (a full run of molding or baseboard, one wall, or an entire window frame) before stopping.
⑤ When doing whole walls, do opposite walls together with the corners of the adjoining walls taped off. After the first pair of walls dries, tape them off and do the second pair.

sponging

Sponging is the simplest of the broken color effects; using a natural sea sponge, the impressions made by its pores when patted on a clean base coat create the effect. Use paint over paint, or glaze over paint, or multiple layers of glazed, sponged effects.

Sponging can be casual and countrified, imitating the look of antique granite – and spongeware. It can be elegantly impressionistic, using several colors of glaze to create an abstract suggestion of a froth of blossoms. In general, large and irregular sponge pores create a more casual appearance; small, uniform pores look light and delicate, suitable for formal spaces.

HOW TO SPONGE

TOOLS:
- One or more natural sea sponges (If a uniform look is desired, examine sponges carefully and pick those with very similar pore size and configuration.)
- Paint tray with disposable tray liner

INGREDIENTS:
- A clean base coat
- Paint or glaze for sponging

1. Tape and mask off areas that will not be painted; apply base coat, and allow to dry thoroughly.
2. Rinse, then wring out the sponge very thoroughly, so it is just moist, not wet.
3. Pour about 1/2" (1 cm) of paint or glaze into paint tray; dip sponge into the paint or glaze lightly, as if you were dipping strawberries into sugar.
4. Blot the sponge lightly on a paper towel or paper plate; then pat it very lightly on the wall. Do not press the sponge to the wall; a light touch gives a more defined impression.
5. Continue sponging in this fashion, remembering to keep the sponge's pores free of paint fragments (examine the sponge frequently and pick off any bits of dried paint.) Continue to keep the sponge lightly moist.
6. Sponging with glaze will produce a translucent pattern; using paint provides an opaque impression. Translucent glaze also combines with the opaque color beneath it; thus the combination of a yellow base with an applied blue glaze sponge pattern will produce green where the two colors overlap. This mixing does not take place when sponging a painted effect with opaque paint.
7. To sponge into corners, try this tip. Instead of using a small version of the sponge used on the walls, use an old paintbrush with splayed bristles. Lightly dip the ends of the bristles into the paint, blot on a paper towel, then touch the brush into the corners with the same light, bouncing motion you use with the sponge.

ragging on/off

Bunched-up rags or plastic bags make wonderful tools for ragging paint or glaze on or off a smooth base coat; the random folds create lively abstract patterns in the paint. Depending upon the material used, the tightness/closeness of the creasing, and the color combination, you can create an infinite number of looks, from soft and casual to restrained and formal.

Ragging on consists of applying paint or glaze to a base coat; ragging off is the process of removing portions of a smooth glaze overcoat by taking up portions of the glaze with crumpled fabric or plastic. Since application techniques are always simpler than subtractive methods, where applied products must be removed, ragging on is easier for the beginner. Like stippling, ragging off is best accomplished with a partner.

HOW TO RAG ON

TOOLS:

- Old, lint free rags, cut up into 20" (51 cm) squares (these can be purchased at paint stores by the box; or, cut up old sheets, or cotton T-shirts.)
- Paint tray and disposable tray liner

INGREDIENTS:

- Good base coat, satin (pearl) or shinier
- Glaze for ragging on

1. After taping and masking off areas that will not be painted, apply smooth base coat and allow to dry thoroughly.
2. To make the ragging tool, scrunch up the rag to the size and shape of a shower pouf; make sure this ball has ridges that will add interest to the ragged effect.
3. Dip the ragging pouf lightly into the paint; blot it on a paper plate or towel so that it isn't drippy.
4. Pounce the ragging pouf *lightly* on the wall. Continue dipping, blotting, and pouncing. This is a randomly patterned effect, so it's all right to go over an area that has already been pounced.
5. Retouching this effect is easy. Simply paint over the area you don't like with the base coat, and reapply glaze with the ragging pouf.

HOW TO RAG OFF

TOOLS:

- A quantity of thin plastic bags (the type used to cover clean clothes at the dry cleaner's is best for fine looks; plastic supermarket or department store bags create a looser appearance.)
- Roller and sleeve with 1/2" (1 cm) nap
- Roller tray and disposable tray liner

INGREDIENTS:

- Good base coat in satin (pearl) or shinier
- Glaze for ragging off (oil-based glaze is best because of its longer working time.)

① Tape off and mask areas that will not be painted; apply base coat and allow to dry thoroughly.

② This effect needs to be done quickly, to keep ahead of drying glaze. As with stippling, work with a partner. One person rolls on the glaze evenly with a lightly loaded roller; the other uses the bunched-up plastic bag to remove glaze; as with most broken color effects, a light touch creates the clearest impression, too much pressure creates smears.

③ After removing glaze, blot it up on a paper towel; when the bag begins to have little bits of glaze start to dry on its surface, discard it and take another clean bag.

④ Keep moving, and keep the pattern connected so there are no lines or blank spaces on the wall. Make sure to work all the glaze as you go, so no large blank spots develop on the wall.

PAINT BOX

Rules for Painting Any Broken Color Effect

KENDALL KLINGBEIL, THE ARTIST WHO PAINTED ALL OF THE EFFECTS IN THIS CHAPTER, OFFERS SEVERAL HARD-AND-FAST RULES FOR GETTING THE BEST RESULTS WHEN PAINTING SPECIAL EFFECTS:

• ALWAYS HAVE LOTS OF PAPER TOWELS ON HAND. USE THE SLIGHTLY MORE EXPENSIVE, CLOTHLIKE BRANDS. THEY WORK BETTER.

• BUY A LITTLE BOX OF LATEX GLOVES (UNLESS YOU ARE ALLERGIC TO THIS SUBSTANCE) TO PROTECT YOUR HANDS WHEN PAINTING, ELIMINATING THE NEED FOR FREQUENT WASHING AND VERY DRY SKIN.

• PRACTICE THE CHOSEN EFFECT ON A PIECE OF BOARD BEFORE APPLYING IT TO THE WALL. IN THIS WAY, YOU CAN CHECK THE COLOR AND TECHNIQUE BEFORE COMMITTING TIME AND ENERGY TO A WHOLE-ROOM PROJECT.

dragging/combing

Similar to a graining effect, a dragging brush or combing tool is pulled through a layer of glaze that has been applied over a smooth base coat.

This action creates a pattern of lines that can be elegant – dragged moldings, cabinets, doors and furniture look very rich – or countrified and casual, depending on the tool used.

Since dragging is done top to bottom or left to right with a stiff-bristled dragging brush, a steady hand is needed to keep the lines going straight.

Dragging and combing are subtractive processes by which glaze is removed with the painting tool, so unless the area being dragged or combed is small and manageable for one person, work with a partner.

HOW TO DRAG/COMB

TOOLS:

- Dragging brush or combing tool
- Roller and sleeve with 1/2″ (1 cm) nap
- Paint tray with disposable tray liner

INGREDIENTS:

- Good base coat with satin (pearl) or shinier paint
- Glaze for dragging (oil base has longer working time)

① Tape and mask off areas not being painted; apply smooth base coat and allow to dry thoroughly.
② Working alone or with a partner, roll on glaze, and immediately draw the dragging brush or the combing tool through the glaze in the desired pattern. After drawing the brush or tool through the glaze, wipe off the tool before dragging again; this prevents excess glaze from building up and making fuzzy, unattractive lines in the paint. When painting cabinets, molding, or furniture, paint in the direction of the wood grain.
③ Be careful of your pressure with the tool at the beginning and end of a dragging or combing line; excessive pressure can cause blurry lines. You may want to practice this technique a few times on sample boards before trying it on a wall or piece of furniture.

stenciling

This is another easy effect, achieved by application rather than subtraction.

While there are hundreds of precut stencils available from commercial manufacturers, making your own is very easy and satisfying. Copy a motif from a favorite fabric, an historical border, even elements of one of your child's drawings, and transform it into a stenciled effect that has personal meaning.

Stencils may be applied with brushes or sponges; the sponged look is a good way to get a subtle stencil image. Because glazes are a bit more slippery than paint, they are not an appropriate medium for filling in a stencil. Use latex or acrylic paint.

MAKE YOUR OWN STENCIL

TOOLS:

- A photocopy or freehand outline of an image you want to use for the stencil; enlarge or reduce the image to the desired size.
- A sheet of clear Mylar or Denril (sold in pads at crafts stores)
- Razor blades, a utility knife, or (best) a stencil burner or woodburning tool with a very fine point
- A fine point marking pen

① Placing the photocopy or freehand outline of your stencil design under a sheet of Mylar or Denril, trace the pattern onto the plastic or, if you are confident with the stencil burner or other cutting tool, simply cut the plastic sheeting along the lines of the pattern, then remove the cutouts. Make multiple copies if a large number of repeats will be needed.

② Stencils can be used for the regular stenciling process; cutouts may be used for reverse stenciling. Both Mylar and Denril are fairly thin, so it should be possible to cut more than one stencil at a time.

NOTE:

When using a stencil burner or cutting tool, work on a fireproof cutting board or a piece of tempered glass.

TO STENCIL

① You will need the stencil, paint, and a tool (brush or sponge) to apply the paint. Choose colors that complement the base; a stencil base can be a smooth coating or a broken color effect. Apply the stencil as a ceiling, wainscot or baseboard border, or as an all-over pattern, like wallpaper.

② If the stencil is compact, just hold it in place while painting over the opening for the design; large or complex designs will need to be positioned with light tack masking tape or repositionable spray adhesive.

TO REVERSE STENCIL

Decide on a motif—leaves, flowers, geometric shapes—and make as many cutouts of these as needed to execute the pattern. Then stick the cutouts in place on a dry, base-coated wall with spray removable adhesive. Paint any applied broken color effect—sponging, stippling, color-washing. Apply the paint right over the cutouts.

When the effect has dried, remove the cutouts, and their pattern will stand out from the broken color effect. This technique looks subtle and lovely when base and broken color hues are closely related.

crackling

Crackling duplicates the alligatored appearance of wood that has layers of paint, cracked from years of repeated exposure to heat, light, and moisture. The aged, distressed appearance of this effect makes it a good choice for country, or colonial, style interiors.

Because crackling medium initiates a chemical process that cannot be controlled, it is somewhat different from other broken color effects. Most home painters will not want to use this product on an entire wall, but crackled moldings, window trim, cabinetry, and shelving can give the patina of age to a room.

HOW TO CRACKLE

TOOLS:

- Bristle brush, sponge brush, or roller

INGREDIENTS:

- Base-coated surface
- Crackling medium
- Latex paint for top layer to be crackled

There is no need to repaint a surface being crackled, as long as the color is satisfactory for an undercoat, and the surface is clean and free of serious flaws.

1. Tape off and mask any areas that will not be crackled.
2. Using a brush, roller, or sponge brush, coat the painted base with crackling medium and allow it to dry; follow manufacturer's instructions. The thicker the application of crackling medium, the more the top layer of paint will crack.
3. Paint the top layer of paint over the crackling medium, and wait.

Cracks will appear as the paint dries, revealing the undercoat and giving the surface a colorful, aged appearance.

marbling

Imitating the look of marble is a great effect wherever marble is logically used in a home — mantels, trim, tabletops. Painting marble on whole walls is not only difficult but looks out of place, except in the most glamorous and luxurious interiors. While it is a somewhat complicated technique, using marbling in a small area makes it easier for one person to complete successfully.

HOW TO MARBLE
Use water-base products for this effect so that there will be less waiting time between layers of paint.

TOOLS:
- Stippling brush
- Rags for ragging on
- Feathers to apply accents (goose or other large bird feathers work well; can be purchased at craft supply stores)

INGREDIENTS:
- A clean, smooth base coat in the appropriate background color (use a piece of real marble as a palette guide, or create your own fantasy marble from favorite colors)
- Three or more shades and tints of latex glazing liquid

① Tape or mask the area the will not be painted; apply base coat and allow to dry thoroughly.
② Apply glaze using a rag on, or rag off over stipple technique to get the cloudy, layered effect that can be seen in marble's surface. Let this layer dry.
③ Apply an additional layer of ragged-on glaze in another color; push it around the surface to imitate the random patterns. Allow this layer to dry.
④ To apply the fine vein lines seen in real marble, dip the edge of a feather in the glaze; it will create a filmy line on the surface. Move the painted feather around and it will create a very natural pattern.
⑤ You may want to experiment with marbling on a practice board before attempting a larger project.

parchment

This is a somewhat advanced applied effect; it is a great technique to use for the look of translucent clouds in the sky. It is an all-paint effect; water-base products will work just fine.

GETTING THE LOOK OF PARCHMENT

TOOLS:

- An old, soft, angled paintbrush works best for this effect

INGREDIENTS:

- Use two closely related tints or shades of latex paint.

① Use a blend of the two colors to paint the smooth base coat; allow paint to dry thoroughly.

② Using the first color, dip the brush into the paint, blot, then press the brush onto the wall with small, circular back-and-forth motions. Work from upper left corner of the wall, across and down.

③ With the second color, repeat the motion, using the same stroke as step 2 and working next to and around the previous strokes.

④ Step back frequently to be sure the effect is not spotty.

⑤ Do one wall at a time, without stopping, so that the look is consistent. This is a physically demanding, energetic painted effect; don't attempt it if you tire easily.

Parchment walls are an extremely elegant look for a foyer, living room, or master bedroom.

PAINT BOX

Tricky Tape

TAPE IS TRICKY; TRY USING BLUE PAINTER'S (LIGHT TACK) TAPE ON A PAINTED SAMPLE BEFORE USING IT TO MASK OFF A BROKEN COLOR EFFECT. OCCASIONALLY THE EFFECT IS FRAGILE AND COMES UP WITH THE TAPE. IT IS MUCH BETTER TO TEST THE TAPE THAN TO RUIN A COMPLICATED PROJECT.

lace effects

Use widths of real lace as reverse stencils to create this fabulous look. It is somewhat costly because of the fabric, but it will make a gorgeous treatment for the wall above a chair rail in a dining room. If you want to moderate the cost, use the look of lace as an accent treatment, on door panels, drawer fronts, or tabletops.

Do not attempt to create lace effects on a wall without help, which you will need to attach the lace to the wall (once spray adhesive goes on, it can stick to itself, or you!)

TOOLS:

• Scissors

• Tape

• Measuring tape

INGREDIENTS:

• A clean, dry base coat

• Sufficient yardage of lace to cover the entire wall area to be treated with a lace effect

• Removable spray adhesive

• Spray paint for reverse stenciling

• Protective clothing (hat, gloves, mask, eye gear)

① Remove the selvage of the lace fabric; then lay out the pattern as you want it to appear on the wall. You may want to tack up the lace to test the look before you stick the fabric down for painting.

② Working with a partner, spray the back of the lace with spray adhesive. Stick lace to the wall from top to bottom, working from the top center out, up, and down, smoothing as you go, until the lace is laid out in the desired pattern.

③ Do not neglect this step! Spray paint casts tiny drops a good distance. Make sure that everything in the room is covered, and block off the doorways to adjoining rooms.

④ Before spray painting the lace, don protective gear so that paint doesn't get into eyes or on skin.

⑤ Spray paint the lace thoroughly; read and follow manufacturers instructions for drying time. When paint is dry, remove the lace.

NOTE:

While painting a whole wall is expensive and a rather difficult procedure, use this idea to create some easier effects. For example, using lace doilies cut in half and positioned along a ceiling, then stencil painted, will create a delightful scalloped lace border for a little girl's or a guest bedroom.

Tools of the Trade

PAINTING ROOMS REQUIRES MANY DECISIONS, BUT SOME THINGS ARE INDISPENSABLE: TO GET

GREAT-LOOKING RESULTS, YOU MUST HAVE THE RIGHT EQUIPMENT. A good place to find out

what you need is the tool kit that a professional painting contractor brings to the job. Take

a look at what's inside:

painting prep equipment

☐ **BASICS**

A DROP CLOTH covers furnishings, rugs, and anything within a room that won't be painted. Use plastic sheets (1 or 2 mils. thick is fine) to cover furnishings; these are available in various sizes, depending on the coverage needed. Invest in a canvas drop cloth for covering floors as you work, particularly if more than one room will be painted; the canvas is sturdier and less slippery than plastic.

AN ALUMINUM-SHADED CLAMP LIGHT with a 100-watt bulb, and a heavy-duty EXTENSION CORD provide the power to illuminate surfaces for smooth wall preparation and thorough paint coverage.

A four- or five-foot (1.2 or 1.5 meter) STEPLADDER will be needed for ceilings eight feet (2.4 meter) or higher. For lower ceilings, a two-foot (0.6 meter) stepladder is easier to move around.

☐ **SMALL PREP TOOLS**

Use flathead and Phillips head SCREWDRIVERS to remove switch and outlet plates and loosen overhead and wall light bases and other hardware from the surfaces that will be painted.

One or more PUTTY KNIVES smooth areas repaired with joint compound or other patching material. These tools are also useful for scraping peeling paint; they come in sizes from one inch wide to more than six inches wide. Wider versions are known as tape knives.

A WIRE BRUSH is good for sweeping away peeling paint from moldings, trim, and around windows. These come in a variety of shapes and sizes.

A UTILITY KNIFE or SCISSORS should be on hand for various cutting chores.

wall prep materials

DRYWALL TAPE is used to join pieces of gypsum wallboard when they are installed. It's also a great product for covering cracks and small holes in the wall surface.

Many painting contractors recommend JOINT COMPOUND for creating a skim coat to smooth over a deteriorated wall, and for patching holes and cracks. They find that premixed joint compound is easier to use than other patching products, such as Spackle, plaster of paris, plaster, or drywall compound.

Buy SANDPAPER in several grit sizes for various smoothing chores. Coarse sandpaper has a grit size of 20-60; medium is 80-150; and fine grit paper is 150 or higher. Sandpaper is available in inexpensive sheets; use lightweight paper for curved surfaces, heavier weight for flat surfaces. For easier handling, spend a bit more and buy sandpaper in sponge or block form.

CAULK is used for filling joints; it can close the gap between sections of molding or baseboard and the wall. Apply it with a CAULKING GUN; follow manufacturer's instructions for using this tool; you may want to practice the technique before using the caulking gun for your paint project.

FOR SAFETY

Clear plastic SAFETY GOGGLES protect eyes from dust and grit, especially when working on overhead areas. A DUST MASK will prevent inhalation of plaster dust and other air-borne particles produced during wall preparation.

Other protective gear includes a PAINTER'S HAT, to keep dust, peeled paint, and liquid paint away from hair. Rather than letting paint touch skin, wear DISPOSABLE GLOVES when working with paint prep products and the paints themselves. Wear old clothing when prepping and painting; if you plan to paint a number of rooms, invest in a pair of painter's pants.

painting equipment

Once the walls have been prepared for painting, assemble the tools for applying paint:

○ **ROLLING TOOLS**

Rolling paint is the fastest way to cover a wall, particularly for a smooth, unbroken finish. To accomplish this, buy a good metal **ROLLER TRAY** that holds the paint; roller tray liners made of plastic eliminate the necessity for heavy cleanup between paint colors. Just dispose of the used liner and pop in a new one for the new color. To spread the paint, select a good quality, sturdy **ROLLER FRAME** and the appropriate sleeves for the job. **ROLLER SLEEVES** (also called roller covers) come in a variety of naps, from short to long. Use the wall surface being covered as the guide to nap length; the smoother the wall surface, the shorter the nap. Synthetic roller sleeves, made of polyester, Dynel, or other manmade fibers, are used with water-based paints. Sleeves made of natural fiber, such as mohair or lamb's wool, are used with oil-based paints. Quality sleeves have thick, dense nap to promote good paint coverage.

For roller-painting ceilings, buy an extension handle for the roller frame; these are available in three- to five-foot (0.9 to 1.5 meter) lengths. The extension handle can also provide additional leverage when running the roller across a surface.

Rollers are a good choice for large, flat areas, but BRUSHES are desirable for places that are not easily rolled: corners, edges, molding, and carved or detailed woodwork. Use brushes with synthetic bristles (nylon or polyester) for water-based products, and brushes with natural bristles for oil-based paints. For brushing paint on broad, flat surfaces, a brush three or more inches wide is desirable; choose one that fits your hand comfortably. For trim and cutting in paint to corners and edges, brushes one to two inches wide with an angled end are often preferred to make this job easier and neater. Some interior painters prefer to use a round sash brush for window trim and small pieces of molding.

When choosing brushes, go for quality. Though premium brushes can be expensive, they will last a long time if properly cleaned and stored (see Paint Practice for cleanup tips.) Before buying a brush, check to see that bristles are secure within the ferrule, the metal band that wraps around them. Brushes with split-bristled, tapered ends hold paint better and ease smooth application. Ruffle through the bristle end with a thumb, and give bristles a slight tug; bristles falling out of a new brush are a sign of poor quality, and stray bristles can ruin a smooth paint job.

PAINTING PADS can be used for covering hard-to-paint places such as the spaces behind pipes, bathroom fixtures, or radiators. Some pads are equipped with angled handles for reaching into tight crevices with the pad.

FOR ANY PAINT JOB

Spills happen. Always have on hand a good supply of PAPER TOWELS and CLEAN RAGS. Keep a household sponge and a BUCKET OF CLEAN WATER on the job site during prep and painting; have the appropriate cleaner for oil-based paints (usually mineral spirits or turpentine; check instructions on the paint label) for cleaning equipment. Since oil-based paints are more difficult to remove from equipment, invest in a brush spinner for the task of keeping the natural bristle brushes used with oils in top condition. Don't forget to pick up a handful of PAINT STIRRING STICKS; retailers usually provide them free of charge.

PAINTER'S TAPE may look like masking tape, but the right product for masking off areas that will not be painted is a light tack product that does not leave its adhesive residue behind. Talk to the paint retailer about the various tapes; one variety of blue tape can be left in place for days and will still be easy to remove. MASKING PAPER, sold in rolls of varying widths, can be used to protect larger areas that will not be painted.

specialized painting tools

Broken color and other special painted effects require specific tools for achieving their distinctive looks. While everything from bunched-up plastic bags to a feather duster can be used to create visual effects in a wet paint medium, these are the tools to create the most popular looks:

☐ **SPONGING**

For applying this decorative effect, NATURAL SPONGES make the best applicators. There are several types of natural sponge, with different pore configurations; some varieties have regularly spaced, even pores, while other sponge surfaces have an irregular combination of large and small pores. Choose a large sponge for the wall, and a smaller sponge of the same variety and pore type for working into corners and tight spots.

PAINT BOX

Using Sponges

NATURAL SPONGES ARE JUST THAT— NATURAL—AND MAY CONTAIN SMALL BITS OF DEBRIS FROM THE OCEAN, THEIR ORIGINAL HOME. ALWAYS RINSE AND THOROUGHLY SQUEEZE OUT A NATURAL SPONGE BEFORE USING IT TO PAINT. ORDINARY CELLULOSE **(KITCHEN) SPONGES** CAN BE USED FOR APPLYING WATER-BASED PAINTS; THESE PROVIDE A MORE OPEN WEB OF PAINT, BUT SHOULD BE CUT INTO IRREGULAR SHAPES TO AVOID LEAVING BEHIND THE ANGULAR MARKS OF AN UNCUT, RECTAN- GULAR SPONGE. SOME **HOME DECORATORS** HAVE USED THE IMPRESSION OF AN UNCUT, RECTANGULAR KITCHEN SPONGE TO REPLI- CATE BRICKS OR BLOCKS ON A WALL MURAL.

Paint Practice

AFTER GATHERING PAINT AND MATERIALS AND SELECTING A COLOR AND TECHNIQUE, THE TIME TO PAINT HAS ARRIVED. This chapter helps organize an approach to room painting to provide great results, with ideas culled from many painting contractors and decorative painters who have long experience in painting practice.

testing color

Nearly every wall needs some preparation before applying paint; repairs and priming are key to the final appearance, and this chapter walks you through the steps for setting up a great base for any paint project. Nonetheless, the time and effort needed for prep work can be trying for do-it-yourselfers who are impatient to see color on the walls. A tiny manufacturer's chip – or even a four by eight (10 cm by 20 cm) sample card – can only provide a hint of how the color will look when painted on the wall. It is a much better strategy to have a little fun and try the color and technique before buying!

COLOR PREVIEW

To serve the very human need for instant gratification, the time before the furniture is moved, drop cloths are draped, and equipment is organized is the perfect occasion to give yourself a preview of the color and technique you have chosen.

TEST SAMPLES

The first step in a great-looking paint job is to create a sample of the smooth or broken color application, and test it in the room you plan to paint. Before purchasing all the paint needed, buy a small sample of the product or products that will be used. The smallest size some manufacturers make for custom color may be a quart, but this experiment may save much more in money and time spent applying several gallons of the wrong custom color!

TEST BOARD

Using a piece of poster board or foam core about eighteen inches by twenty-four inches (46 cm by 61 cm), paint the color directly on the board, using the technique that will be applied to the walls. Once the color is dry, take a day or two to live with the color; see how it looks at different times of day, bathed in the natural and artificial light that normally illuminates the room.

CHECKING THE HUE

Move the board around; place it in a doorway and approach it from another room or area of the house, to see how the new hue works with visible colors in adjacent rooms. With this experiment, using a sample while the furnishings are in place, it becomes much easier to see whether or not the color and application are right for the space.

PAINT BOX

Testing Your Colors

WHEN USING SEVERAL COLORS, PAINT ONE BOARD IN EACH COLOR TO BE USED IN THE ROOM, AND POSITION THE BOARDS WHERE THE COLOR WILL BE PAINTED.

A DESIGNER'S TRICK FOR JUDGING THE BALANCE BETWEEN COLORS IS TO CREATE THE BOARDS IN PROPORTION TO THE AMOUNT OF SURFACE THEY WILL COVER.

THUS, A SAMPLE BOARD OF **TRIM COLOR** THAT REPRESENTS ABOUT TWENTY-FIVE PERCENT OF THE SPACE IN THE ROOM SHOULD BE ONLY ONE-QUARTER OF THE TOTAL SIZE OF THE SAMPLE BOARDS — WHEN THE TWO BOARDS ARE PLACED SIDE BY SIDE, IT BECOMES EASIER TO SEE HOW THEY WILL ULTIMATELY WORK TOGETHER.

---

prepping the room

Once color and technique are decided, take these steps to get ready to prime and paint.

☐ **WALLS**

- Before moving any furniture, appraise the walls in bright light; use sticky notes or pencil marks to indicate wall flaws that will need special prepping with sanding or joint compound. A clamp light with an aluminum shade provides strong illumination to make this task simpler. This step is particularly important when the final finish needs to be smooth and glossy; once the paint is on the walls, the flaws will ruin an otherwise great paint job.

☐ **SET-UP**

- Remove all fragile knick-knacks, place remaining furniture in the center of the room, and roll up area rugs. Cover furniture with a plastic drop cloth; if you have one, use a canvas drop cloth for the floor. Otherwise use a thick plastic one or large sheets of brown paper.

☐ **SWITCH PLATES**

- Remove the decorative plates that cover switches and wall outlets; loosen light fixtures and protect them with masking paper (or cover with plastic or paper bags).

☐ **TOOLS**

- Gather all prep tools and put them on a table (protect the table first with a drop cloth or a piece of flattened corrugated box); the table can be the central base of operations, so tools don't get lost. Or put everything together in one central spot on the floor. Don't forget to watch your step!

preparing surfaces

If walls are new or fairly smooth, the prepping should go quickly. Loose paint or plaster can be removed with a putty or tape knife. Screw holes or taped seams should be filled with joint compound or other repair medium. Once the filler dries (follow directions for drying time carefully),

the surface can be sanded smooth. Unless rough, distressed walls are desirable for the final finish, remember that a smooth base is a must for achieving a polished paint job.

☐ **COMMON REPAIRS**

Attend to nicks, dents, cracks, and spaces between walls and molding; these problems constitute the major repairs before painting walls.

☐ **FILL GAPS**

After scraping loose paint or removing flakes of plaster, the next step is to fill in any gaps and indentations with the chosen compound – plaster, joint compound, and drywall compound, plaster of paris, or Spackle. Apply the selected product with a putty or tape knife; wipe the knife clean between each pass on the wall surface, and the work will progress more quickly.

☐ **CAULK CRACKS**

For spaces between walls and trim or baseboards, caulk may be preferable to other repair media, as it can be applied with a caulking gun to fill in these narrow spaces, and the excess wiped away with a sponge.

☐ **SAND SURFACES**

Always follow manufacturer's instructions for drying time of any repair compounds. Once all repaired surfaces are thoroughly dried, they may be sanded smooth. Give plenty of attention to smoothing window trim and moldings; since these surfaces are often painted in flaw-revealing, glossy paints, extra care will ensure the best result.

PAINT BOX

Lighten Your Load

FULL PAINT CANS ARE HEAVY! USE EMPTY PAINT BUCKETS OR CLEAN COFFEE CANS FOR HOLDING PAINT WHEN WORKING ON THE CEILING, TRIM, OR MOLDINGS; POUR A SMALL QUANTITY FROM THE LARGE CAN INTO THE BUCKET OR COFFEE CAN.

PAINT BOX

About Lead Paint

SEVENTY-FIVE PERCENT OF HOMES BUILT BEFORE THE LATE 1970S MAY HAVE LEAD PAINT ON WALLS AND TRIM. IF YOU LIVE IN A **HOME THAT PREDATES 1978**, WHEN THE USE OF LEAD WAS BANNED AS THE HIDING PIGMENT IN PAINT, ONE OR MORE LAYERS OF EXISTING PAINT MAY CONTAIN LEAD. IF THE PAINT SURFACE IS IN GOOD CONDITION, SIMPLY PRIME AND PAINT. HOWEVER, IF THERE IS DETERIORATION OF THE PAINT SUBSTRATES, WITH PEELING AND FLAKING (A PARTICULAR PROBLEM AROUND EXTERIOR WINDOWS AND DOORS), **DO NOT DRY SCRAPE OR DRY SAND THESE AREAS,** FOR THE ENSUING DUST COULD CONTAMINATE LARGE AREAS OF THE HOME. LEAD DUST IS TOXIC, PARTICULARLY TO SMALL CHILDREN.

IF YOU SUSPECT A LEAD PROBLEM, GET THE FACTS BEFORE PAINTING. INFORMATION ABOUT LEAD PAINT, LEAD ABATEMENT, AND OTHER MEANS OF CONTAINING A LEAD PAINT PROBLEM ARE AVAILABLE THROUGH CONTACTS LISTED IN THE RESOURCES SECTION.

The Order of Painting Rooms

TO GET THE BEST POSSIBLE RESULT, FOLLOW THE PAINTING ORDER USED BY PROFESSIONALS FOR PRIMING AND PAINTING THE ROOM:

1. **CEILINGS**
2. **WALLS**
3. **TRIM**
4. **WINDOWS AND DOORS**
5. **BASEBOARDS**

CLEANING UP

Prep work can leave behind a residue of dust over the wall surface; before applying primer or paint, do not neglect to clean all the prepared surfaces. Vacuum the walls, clean them with a tack cloth, or wash them so that no residue remains. Be sure all surfaces are thoroughly dry before priming or painting.

applying color

Now comes the fun part: applying the colors and techniques you have chosen to enliven your rooms. Though it may be difficult to contain your excitement, remember that you have given this decorating process much time and thought; it will be worth your time if you execute your plan carefully.

PRIMING

With the exception of raw wood to which milk paint is being applied, most surfaces will need a priming coat to help the smooth base coat of color adhere to the surface and dry to perfection. Nearly every manufacturer makes primers that pair with their paints for good adhesion and successful results.

☐ **OIL-BASED VS. WATER-BASED PRIMERS**
In general, oil primers should be used with oil-based paints, and water-based primers applied as the undercoat for latex and acrylic paint products.

☐ **PRIMER AND SURFACE**
Different primers prepare different surfaces; special priming products exist for every kind. For your painting project, consult the paint manufacturer's instructions, and the paint dealer, to get the right priming product for the job. As with all paints, adhere carefully to the specified drying times for primers; coating a still-damp, primed wall with paint can cause all kinds of problems.

☐ **PAINTING CEILINGS**
Because ceiling drips can do damage to the rest of the room, be sure that all areas below the ceiling are covered with drop cloths or masked. Don't forget the tops of doors, interior shutters, or wall-mounted fixtures.

☐ **ROLLER WORK**
Roller work should proceed in roughly three-foot by three-foot (0.9 by 0.9 meter) areas for the best coverage. Starting from one corner, mentally divide your ceiling space into segments of this size, working back and forth across the room. After thoroughly stirring the paint, and using a liner in the roller tray, pour paint from the can into the tray, to a depth of about an inch (3 cm) in the deep section of the tray. Fill the roller sleeve with paint and roll it back and forth in the tray so it is fully coated but not drippy.

HOW TO ROLL

First, roll the paint in a rough "W" across the
first area. Then, without adding more paint, roll
out the painted "W" over the three-foot (0.9
meter) section. Continue this process until the
whole ceiling is painted. Be sure that the area is
well lighted, and examine the work in progress.

MISSED SPOTS

Do not add paint when a spot is missed;
smoothing over can be done with a dry roller
sleeve so fresh paint is not added to a spot
that is already drying.

COVERAGE

While flat finish, white ceiling paint usually
provides good coverage in a single coat, allow
the paint to dry before deciding on a second
coat. If a special effect will be used on the ceiling,
complete it before beginning to paint the walls.

PAINTING WALLS

Once the neck-cramping work of ceiling painting
is finished, the walls come next.

MASKING

If the ceiling is white, and the wall will be painted
in a different color, mask the edge of the ceiling
before doing the wall brushwork. Mask trim,
window, and door edges, and the tops of baseboards, unless these will be done in the same
shades and gloss as the walls.

EDGES AND FIXTURES

Use the same techniques as with the ceiling,
cutting in with a brush at edges and around
fixtures and outlets. Then roll in three-foot by
three-foot sections, working top to bottom,
left to right, one wall at a time.

PAINTING DETAILS

Decorative trim around ceiling edges, as well
as windows, doors, and baseboards often gets
special treatment with a higher-gloss finish
than walls and ceiling, because they are most
vulnerable to dirt, finger marks, and other
blemishes that will need regular cleaning.

CONTRASTING COLORS

Painting these details in contrasting or complementary colors can also be an effective strategy
for giving a room definition and refinement. In
either case, the work should be carefully done.

DETAIL MASKING

Mask the line between trim, moldings, baseboards
or windows, and the adjoining walls. Burnish the
tape with a blunt instrument (a putty knife or
similar tool) so that paint will not seep underneath the tape. Be sure that the floor beneath
the painting area is protected by newspaper or
drop cloth from drips, spills, and spatters.

PAINTING DOORS

When painting doors, many pros just remove
hardware, rather than masking it, as many
metallic knobs and locks are now coated with
finishes that can be ruined by cleaning with
anything stronger than water. This eliminates
the need to cut in paint around knobs and
latches, making the job go more quickly.

PAINTING WINDOWS

Anyone who has ever painted a room will
acknowledge that painting windows, especially
those with many small panes of glass, is a
particular challenge.

Here are some recommendations from the pros:

When painting double hung windows, paint the
outer sash first. Keep both sashes open, and
apply paint in a thin layer. Move the window up
and down as painting proceeds, so that neither
sash gets painted shut. When painting the thin
wood bars around the panes (called muntins),
some professionals recommend that these
parts be painted without masking the glass.

SCRAPING VS. MASKING

Paint that gets onto glass can be easily removed
by scraping with a razor blade, provided paint
removal is done soon after the paint dries. Pros
note that masking, and then removing tape from
these small spaces, can be more time-consuming
than just scraping away the drips from the
glass. Tape that stays on too long (except for
blue painter's tape) can leave a gummy residue
more difficult to remove than dripped paint!

finishing the job

After painting, examine the whole job in good, bright light before putting away equipment and cleaning up. Look for any areas the paintbrush missed, and fill them in. When the paint has dried thoroughly, scrape off any drips and spatters with a razor blade, sand them smooth, clean the dust, and retouch.

☐ **DISPOSAL**

Remove all masking tape and clean equipment (soap and water for latex, mineral spirits or manufacturer-specified cleaner for alkyd). Empty latex paint cans can be allowed to dry, then tossed out (Do not throw liquid paint in the trash.) Dispose of alkyds, their containers and tools according to local hazardous waste disposal rules (There are usually special collection days or disposal centers.)

HOW TO GET THE PERFECT COLOR

Decorating rooms with paint requires a synergy of skills. Buying the right products, in the right colors, and using them artfully to achieve a desired effect. In the following section, readers can see beautiful effects with paint-finished rooms and decorative vignettes that reveal harmonious relationships of color, architecture, and furnishings; they succeed aesthetically. But more importantly, *Painting Your House Inside and Out* takes the extra step to tell the reader why they work so well.

Successful palettes encompass the relationships of colors to each other, to the furnishings they surround, to light streaming from windows and from interior sources, to the needs and tastes of the people who dwell within the spaces. Some understanding of all these relationships will enable any do-it-yourselfer to choose color more confidently.

The text for this section offers guidance for painting with each major color of the spectrum, and includes the use of neutrals. It provides pointers for observing and selecting the shades, tints, and special effects that capture inspirations culled from nature and daily living – the sources for most decorating ideas. This section offers recommendations for combining a favorite color with other hues that will enhance and complement that color. It divulges tips from professional designers and painters, whose years of experience can add to the reader's repertoire of skills. So, whether your favorite vase or the color in a summer sunset inspires you to paint, this section contains ample instruction for putting a chosen hue to work to create a beautiful interior.

Painting with Blue

SO EASY ON THE EYE, THE WINNER OF EVERY COLOR POPULARITY CONTEST, BLUE IS A VERSATILE PERFORMER IN THE HOME PAINT PALETTE. THE SERENE, THOUGHT-PROVOKING QUALITY OF THIS HUE SETS A TRANQUIL TONE FOR WORK, STUDY, AND REST, MAKING BLUE AN APPEALING CHOICE FOR KITCHENS, HOME OFFICES, BEDROOMS, AND BATHS. As useful in the home's public spaces as it is in private ones, blue can easily serve as a key decorating color for an entire home.

Blue has many positive associations; blue chips are the best stocks, blue ribbons the top awards. This prized connotation has a long history; before the invention of synthetic pigment, blue was made by grinding precious stones to powder. Ultramarine blue was made in this fashion and used sparingly by artists to depict the heavens and other lofty subjects. Today, modern manufacturers provides us with an enormous range of blues to match every decorating inspiration, in products accessible to all.

Pale blue walls make a good backdrop for natural wood furniture; the pale orange tone of the wood is a natural complement in the spectrum to light blue. Old washboards painted in the other primary hues show how a muted primary scheme works well in this country setting.

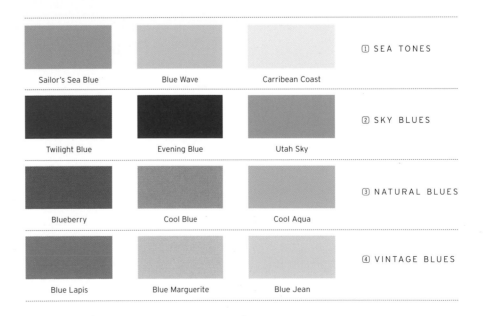

Sailor's Sea Blue	Blue Wave	Carribean Coast	① SEA TONES
Twilight Blue	Evening Blue	Utah Sky	② SKY BLUES
Blueberry	Cool Blue	Cool Aqua	③ NATURAL BLUES
Blue Lapis	Blue Marguerite	Blue Jean	④ VINTAGE BLUES

Even without the harbor view, pale blue-gray walls enhance the contemplative feeling of this room under the eaves. White trim amplifies the color's depth and complexity. White furnishings and pale floors mirror the room's subdued tone, and dark wood accessories, such as the graphically strong, thumb-back Windsor chair, have been added to stand out in the soft surroundings. Touches of primary bright color make good accents in this room; note how the red journal pops out among all the receding tones.

According to formalized color theory, the natural complement of blue on the spectrum is orange. Paint a room using these two colors together to create an appealing harmony; note the pleasing effect when polished, reddish-orange colored wood furniture such as maple or mahogany is paired with blue walls.

Putting aside the theoretical, look for good partners for blue by observing it in nature. Many blue flowers have white or yellow centers; look for blue/white or blue/yellow combinations on the following pages and see how well they work.

Another surprisingly effective complement for blue is green. Observing blue flowers surrounded by their green leaves and stems proves the point; a green couch or chair in front of a blue painted wall makes the same, harmonious statement. Many shades of blue work well together in a monochromatic scheme. Should this decorative pattern prove a bit chilly, it can quickly be warmed with a few accents, such as decorative pillows or tabletop objects in the primary colors of red and yellow.

sea and sky effects

Few things are as soothing to the soul as an afternoon at the beach spent gazing at the ever-changing sea, where the colors constantly shift in response to weather, wind, and the angle of the sun. To capture the colors of the water and sky in your home, observe the play of light in the rooms to be painted. The quality of the light at the time of day a space is used determines whether a sparkling, light-struck blue, a pale gray-blue, or a deep, saturated tone is most appropriate. In general, paint morning-lit spaces with clear blues. For rooms usually illuminated by incandescent lights, use different shades of blue.

PAINTING WITH SEA TONES

Rooms for contemplation and rest, such as a bedroom, home office, sun porch or spa bathroom, benefit from colors blended in warm sea tones. Light colorwashes or sponged patterns of blue green over a lighter ground provide a subtle and soothing backdrop for quiet or solitary activity. Look at marine paintings, and notice that the artist will usually employ many colors to create the play of light on water. Replicate this dynamic effect with multiple layers of color that are applied by colorwashing, stippling, or sponging; use a pale gray/light blue, and finish with a slightly darker blue or blue-green. Such an effect will provide depth and complexity to walls in hallways, powder rooms, or other spaces that have simple, or few, furnishings. Single layers of color also evoke the sea's many moods. The ocean in late afternoon, when the low angle of the sun or rolling fog dims the sparkly surface, often pales to a soft gray-blue, a tranquil tone appropriate for a quiet sitting room, office, or meditation space.

*Recreate the tranquil tones of a
landscape by the sea with walls
colorwashed in a coastal blue
over raw, rough plaster. The
blue-white palette carried
throughout the room creates a
serene, cooling effect in a space
designed for summer dreaming.*

Painting a light-struck stairway in the colors of sky and clouds creates a dramatic, celestial effect for those who climb the steps.

APPLYING SKY BLUES

Consider painting a ceiling in a refreshing alternative to plain white-blue hues that suggest a clear daytime sky. Puffy, cloudlike patterns applied by rag-rolling, stippling, sponging, or even stenciling, on a sky-blue ceiling create a floating sensation for the child or adult gazing upward at this effect. While clouds typically decorate a bedroom or nursery ceiling, they might also comfortably grace the upper reaches of sitting rooms, libraries, and other spaces where people relax. On walls, apply sky tints to create a feeling of vertical movement in a home. Picture a stairway with steps in natural wood complemented by sky-blue risers; they move upward to a landing with the walls painted in the same blue. This produces an almost celestial effect, especially if there is sun streaming in through a window or skylight.

NIGHT-SKY EFFECTS

Walls or ceilings that capture the look of a night sky provide an intimate enclosure for a bedroom, study, or other cozy space. Dark, deep blues such as navy, midnight, lapis lazuli, or indigo can be dramatic and luxurious. In a hallway or den, use a glossy or glazed dark blue finish that reflects lamplight to make the space seem rich and elegant, particularly if the walls are hung with pictures in gilded frames. Another dramatic look is a deep blue ceiling, stenciled with small white or gilded stars, lit from below by wall sconces or lamps. Since dark paint will make a ceiling seem lower, painting one in deep blue is an effective remedy for high or vaulted ceilings.

using natural blues

Look to the natural world for an infinite selection
of inspirations. The iridescent glow of a dragonfly,
the cheerful hue of a bluebird, the delicate tint of
a blue crab's shell as it skitters along the rocks at
water's edge — all these creatures brighten their
surroundings, just as their colors would enliven a
room. The garden is also a source for brilliant
blues to paint in a decorating scheme. Use the
spectacularly bright hue of a delphinium or bache-
lor's button to paint cabinets, architectural details,
or trim in kitchens or baths equipped with lots of
white. Although white connotes cleanliness and
good hygiene, too much white in an already bright
space promotes glare; eye-soothing blue makes an
excellent complement.

The frosty rime on a blueberry or juniper berry
gives the fruit a powdery appearance that belies
its juiciness. This muted blue makes a great wall
color that enhances the look of natural wood.
Think of it for a dining area or any seating space
filled with natural-toned furniture.

painting with vintage blue

Glittering blue-green prisms in a vintage chandelier inspired the satiny walls of this long corridor, hung with framed prints, photographs, and mirrors that capture and reflect the light.

Few ceramic patterns are as recognizable as the blue-gray dishes and cups, decorated with classical designs in white relief, first made by potter Josiah Wedgwood in the eighteenth century. This distinctive blue jasperware has been an inspiration for many blue-decorated rooms ever since.

Many vintage blues are distinguished by their shading; important rooms at Colonial Williamsburg, as well as the country blue of many historic Scandinavian interiors, have a touch of gray. Such subtle, light-enhancing color provides a delicate aspect to rooms that are furnished with elegant, fine-boned furniture, or bleached or natural-toned floors, for an overall pastel feeling.

PAINT BOX

Accentuating with Paint

USE PAINT TO ACCENTUATE SPECIAL FEATURES OF VINTAGE ROOMS. FOR EXAMPLE, APPLY PAINT IN A STRONGER SHEEN FOR DECORATIVE MOLDINGS AND SURFACES IN RELIEF TO HIGHLIGHT THESE ARCHITECTURAL DETAILS, SINCE COLOR LOOKS MORE VIBRANT IN A GLOSSY OR SEMIGLOSS FINISH THAN IN MATTE OR EGGSHELL SHEEN. ONE OF THE LOVELIEST FINISHES IN VINTAGE COUNTRY HOUSES IS MILK-BASED PAINT. THE EARTHY PIGMENTS AND SOFT MATTE SHEEN MAKE A WONDERFUL COUNTERPOINT TO COLORFULLY PAINTED OR DISTRESSED, FARMHOUSE-STYLE FURNISHINGS. BLUE MILK PAINT IS AVAILABLE IN A LIGHT BLUE TONED WITH GRAY, AS WELL AS A RICH DARK BLUE, DUBBED "HEAVENLY" BY THE SHAKERS, PLUS CUSTOM TINTS OR SHADES IN BETWEEN. MILK-BASED PAINT HAS A SOFT FINISH, WHICH CAN BE MARRED BY BUMPING FURNITURE OR EVEN SPLASHING LIQUID. PROTECT IT WITH A COAT OF CLEAR WAX.

Vivid primary blue walls and stairs stained an equally bright yellow combine for a striking palette in this vintage farmhouse room. While milk paints in more muted shades are a standard treatment in antique homes, using intense hues adds contemporary flavor to classic styles.

Painting with Red

RED GETS NOTICED. JUST AS THE DAMSEL IN THE SCARLET DRESS ATTRACTS EVERY EYE IN THE ROOM, ROOMS PAINTED RED HAVE A NATURAL MAGNETISM, MAKING THIS A LOGICAL COLOR CHOICE FOR ANY SPACE WHERE PEOPLE GATHER – ENTRYWAYS, LIVING AND DINING ROOMS. Red makes such a memorable statement that one of its many tints and shades finds its way into almost every home palette. Use red's dramatic flair by painting it on a single wall in an otherwise neutral-colored space. This strategy works to highlight any objects or furnishings placed on or in front of the red wall, creating an instant focal point. Painting a single surface to stand out is a contemporary treatment, particularly effective when interior architecture consists of smooth planes without trim and molding details.

Blushing Bride	Delicate Rose	Early Sunrise	① PASTEL REDS
Chili Pepper	Tomato Red	Berry Wine	② GOURMET REDS
Million Dollar Red	Red	Red Tulip	③ JEWEL TONE REDS
Raisin Torte	Confederate Red	Bull's Eye Red	④ WINE REDS

Strong patterns, textures, and decorative objects blend in a rich harmony when surrounded by walls in the shade of fine red wine. The deep claret tone mutes a disparate collection of exotic furnishings for an effect that is inviting and supremely comfortable.

When considering which colors work best with red, picture a bouquet of long-stemmed red roses or a vase of red Emperor tulips. Their green foliage creates harmonious surroundings for the brilliant red flowers. Similarly, green — red's complement — can work as a trim or carpet color in rooms with red walls; think green with a bit of yellow for deep-toned reds, and green with a dash of blue for more orangey reds. Observe other red flowers and their foliage for additional, appealing red-and-green combinations.

Red also creates a related color scheme in rooms with natural wood detailing — molding, doors, and cabinetry, which, in their unpainted state have a somewhat orange hue. Walls can be painted in an unbroken, matte finish for a cozy appearance, or colorwashed for a lighter, country feeling. Complete this scheme with accents close to red on the spectrum — red-violet, or yellows with a touch of red in them.

Language scholars note that red is the first color to receive a name in nearly every culture, and child development specialists have determined that red is the hue that a baby's eyes will target in his early glimpses of the world. This primitive connection to red makes it a natural choice for the décor in children's rooms, though it need not be confined to a scheme of primary colors. Use red as a key color in a painted wall mural, or as a stenciled border of silhouettes just below the ceiling. Sponge on red over a light background for a bright but subdued wall treatment, reminiscent of the sponge-decorated pottery that brightens many country-style homes.

pastel red: painting with pink

Young women often have their first experience with pastel red in the hospital nursery, where girls are swaddled in pink blankets. Thus this pale tint has a common association with little girls' bedrooms and all things frilly and feminine. Yet pink performs well beyond this narrow decorating pigeonhole. Pink walls create softly illuminated social and workspaces, such as living rooms, libraries, or offices, where furnishings bask in its flattering light.

Pastel pink can range from cool — touched with a bit of blue — to a warmer hue with a slightly yellowed tone that moves the resulting color toward coral and other seashell tints. The intensity and source of light that shines on pink walls and other pale-painted surfaces will make a significant difference in how the color is perceived. Intense sunlight can overheat warm pink, and conversely, dim light can make cool pink look drab. Although people fret more about the final appearance of very dark or bright colors, their pallor disguises the trickiness of pastels. Since pale tints contain a significant percentage of white in their mix, the resulting color will have the light-reflecting quality of white paint. To gauge a pastel's appropriateness for a particular room, always take the intermediate step of testing the chosen hue with a large sample board, paying particular attention to the color as it appears when exposed to all the room's light sources.

Not just for frilly bedrooms, pink walls enliven formal spaces as well. Complemented by quantities of greenery and light-catching crystal chandeliers, this pastel sitting room creates a harmony of softly elegant texture and light.

Windowless kitchens, and those with wide expanses of white, sometimes have a hard, high-tech quality that needs some colorful relief for the eye. Here, raspberry walls contrast with bright white equipment, while enhancing the soft sheen of stainless steel fixtures and kitchen tools.

PAINT BOX

Disguising Less-than-Perfect Walls

RED ROOMS LOOK RICH AND ELEGANT WHEN THE WALLS ARE GLAZED IN A MODERATE TO HIGH SHEEN, YET A SHINY, SMOOTH COATING ALSO DRAWS ATTENTION TO FLAWS IN THE SURFACE. TO DISGUISE LESS-THAN-PERFECT WALLS, USE A BROKEN PAINT TECHNIQUE SUCH AS SPONGING OR RAG ROLLING, WHICH GIVES THE PAINTED SURFACE DIMENSION AND DEPTH WHILE CONCEALING MINOR DEFECTS.

applying gourmet reds to rooms

So many red foods exist in the natural world that manufacturers have taken this cue and lined the grocery shelves with thousands of packages that feature red graphics and images. Its mouth-watering quality makes red an excellent color choice in rooms designated for eating and socializing. Such a colorful stimulant will make dining rooms, kitchens, and entertaining spaces as lively as the guests within.

Not everyone thinks of red for the kitchen, as its assertiveness might be just too much excitement at breakfast. Yet one of the cooler reds – shades with a bit of blue in them – creates a wonderful contrast with the large expanses of white cabinets and appliances so popular in contemporary kitchens. This juxtaposition seems to relax the sharpness of raspberry red or cerise, while softening the austere brightness of white fixtures and furnishings. Any workspace – kitchen, laundry, even the home office – with a monotone scheme, whether white, beige, gray or tan, feels more comfortable when these fruity reds are added to the palette.

Shades of spicy red work extremely well in rooms occupied in the evening hours; candles and other indirect lighting patterns serve to increase their friendly glow. Many decorators like to specify one of the rich shades of red for dining rooms, as this color not only whets the appetite for food, but also provides a rosy background that makes a room's occupants look their best.

USING RED DETAILS

A luscious sundae bedecked with whipped cream and a single, glossy maraschino cherry makes a great analogy for the way in which bright red works as an accent color in rooms. Use high-gloss red – the color of toy wagons and shiny fire engines – to bring forward architectural details in rooms painted white, cream, or other neutral colors. For a crisp, finished look, pick out elements such as trim, cabinet knobs, and the outline molding of raised paneling. Such a treatment enhances the happy, lively look of children's rooms, where red trim completes a polished, primary scheme in a white-walled space with blue and yellow furnishings.

applying jewel-tone reds

The red of precious and semiprecious stones is a
clear, sparkling shade that radiates warmth. Use it
for a glowing sitting room that no one will want to
leave, or as a welcoming embrace in a front hallway.
White trim, or white upholstered furniture, tone
down the brightness of jewel reds while maintaining
an overall look of sophisticated comfort. A bright
red room can be the exclamation point in an otherwise subdued home palette; chances are, it will
also be the space that guests will remember best.

using the shades of red wine

In the glass, a fine red wine sometimes looks
brown, or almost black; held up to the light, the
depth of its crimson glow becomes apparent. This
corresponds to the transformation of deep, dark
red walls when they are illuminated. Deep reds
have long been used on walls to mimic the effect
of fine wood paneling, a painted treatment that is
enhanced by architectural features such as applied
molding and raised panels. Dragging a coat of
darker red over a lighter red can provide more of
the appearance of wood grain; finished with a coat
of clear glaze, walls look lustrous and rich by lamp
or candlelight.

Because iron oxide is a pigment accessible to
almost every culture, dark reds have not been
reserved for faux-wood treatments in elegant dining rooms. Palettes for farmhouses around the
world contain some version of the dark reds drawn
from local clays and sediments. For country houses,
red-brown paint can color moldings, doors and
other wood trim, cabinets in a farmhouse kitchen,
or stencils across a raw plaster wall. This color
combines with all types of wood for a soft, warm
monochromatic scheme, and creates a lovely
backdrop for rustic painted furniture and folk art
accessories. Use milk paint for its soft and authentic country look, or acrylic paint in a flat finish, to
duplicate the vintage, matte appearance.

*Walls colorwashed in a deep
farmhouse red conform to the
rustic flavor of a dining room
furnished with treasured finds
from country auctions and flea
markets. Using the rich, dark
tones provided by old-fashioned,
natural earth pigments is an
authentic and historically accurate wall treatment for antique
houses in rural settings.*

Ruby red walls demonstrate the power of a bright color to illuminate a small space. The homeowners have made this formal room the centerpiece of their apartment, which is painted in a palette of primary hues. The tricolor scheme is successful for several reasons. While the red is an intense shade, yellow and blue walls have lighter values, so the resulting scheme is harmonious and eye-pleasing. Notice also how white is used as a unifying trim color, to separate the hues and enhance their clarity.

Painting with Yellow

IF COLOR IS LIGHT MADE VISIBLE, THEN YELLOW IS THE BRIGHTEST LIGHT IN THE SPECTRUM. THINK OF A PROCESSION OF YELLOW RAINCOATS STREAMING OUT OF THE LOCAL ELEMENTARY SCHOOL ON A RAINY MARCH MONDAY—HOW THEY CHEER THE LANDSCAPE AND THE HEARTS OF EVERYONE WHO SEES THEM. Such is the uplifting effect of yellow, and a perfect reason to paint with it somewhere in a home's interior. Yellow paint brightens a windowless hallway or a dimly lit room under the eaves; it is sunshine in a can. Apply intense, golden yellow as a trim color in a dark-paneled, rustic den; glossy details pop out from the subdued background. Then pick up the yellow accent in decorative details: a woven throw, pillows, or a bowl of golden delicious apples.

Banana Yellow	Bright Yellow	Lemon	① BRIGHT YELLOW
Lemon Freeze	Lemon Meringue	Light Daffodil	② PALE AND SOFT YELLOWS
Golden Nugget	Sunshine	Yellow Raincoat	③ SPICY YELLOW

Two shades of golden yellow—a lighter base with a darker layer of glaze ragged off—create a glowing setting for casual and memorable meals. This treatment gives ordinary sheetrock walls the textured appearance of stucco, and creates a rustic background for contemporary decorative objects and art.

Lemon yellow walls enhance this kitchen's spacious dimensions. Use expanses of white, plus wood floors and furnishings, to temper the impact of this strong hue. Decorate with bright accents, such as the flowers and abstract prints, as they seem to glow more brightly against the sunny background.

High-gloss yellow paint, a staple for kitchens and baths where brightness is a plus, reflects light like no other hue in the spectrum. Apply shiny treatments in yellow wherever more light and good washability are important: home offices, play rooms, family rooms, hallways leading to private sections of the home. Use bulbs labeled "warm" in fluorescent fixtures to avoid any possible greenish glare.

Yellow provides a pleasing background in rooms with plentiful live greenery and good natural light: enclosed sun porches, breakfast rooms, or any space constructed around a greenhouse window. Colorwash yellow over a lighter ground such as white or ivory, to create an air of soft informality in such indoor/outdoor spaces.

A natural choice for morning-lit bedrooms and kitchens, yellow walls make great surroundings for waking up, or the first cup of coffee. Striping or sponging yellow on white walls in a bedroom will immediately energize the surroundings. Yellow combines harmoniously with so many other colors that few changes in decorative accessories will be needed.

Because of its inherent brightness, yellow may be applied in rooms of all sizes, from cavernous to compact. A monochromatic scheme, using two or three tints or shades of yellow, creates a cheerful, sociable space. Monet's dining room at Giverny is such a two-toned testimonial to the power of yellow, and no one who sees it forgets its brilliant beauty.

painting with bright yellow

Tropical yellows—the colors of ripe bananas, lemons, or a toucan's beak—look lively paired with white trim, or accompanied by other hues from southern latitudes, such as hot pink, mango, or turquoise. While these combinations are most at home in climates where palm trees thrive, high-voltage colors can also work under cooler northern light, particularly when their intensity is tempered by expanses of white or light neutral colors. In a kitchen, this means lemon yellow walls with white cabinets—or the reverse. In a bright yellow bedroom, aqua accents and off-white trim and linens can tone down this energizing hue.

Primary yellow walls create a happy setting for a child's bedroom or playroom; complement this sun-bright look with a pale blue ceiling sponged with clouds. Or, if the ceiling is high and the child is a budding astronomer, create a night sky above the yellow walls, accented with tiny, glow-in-the-dark stars. Using the sky image on ceilings will mitigate yellow's energizing property at bedtime, creating a peaceful feeling when young ones gaze upward from their pillows.

The bright yellow of egg yolks or sunflowers can also renew and revive a dated kitchen, when applied in a discernible sheen, from satin to high-gloss, on kitchen cabinets. Add new hardware and window treatments to complete a very cheery and cost-effective rehab of older stained-wood cabinets.

Revive a dated kitchen by painting old wood cabinets and adding new hardware. Here, butter yellow cabinets in a glossy finish are paired with lavender-blue walls, providing a cheerful country setting for cooking and dining.

using pale yellow

A pastel tinted yellow glaze over a white, ivory or beige base achieves subtle effects that gently illuminate rooms. Walls that are sponged, rag-rolled or stippled in this fashion provide the illusion of sunlight through sheer curtains on walls. While the combination of white and yellow is a traditional pairing, increase the color value by using other pastels as complements. Pale violet upholstery looks luscious against yellow walls; pale pink or robin's egg blue can also make refined partners for this hue. A pastel scheme brightens dim interior rooms, and looks especially refreshing with pale wood furnishings.

painting with soft shades of yellow

The most gently sparkling jewel in the spectrum of gems, topaz has a subdued yellow tone that adds a dignified glow to walls when used as a paint color. Yellow toned down with a dab of gray and warmed with a touch of red has an elegant appearance that pairs well with formal furnishings. It creates a subdued undertone when used in broken color treatments – as the undercoat for a blue-green crackle finish, or the base coat for red glaze dragged over moldings, doors and window trim. Topaz is the color of late afternoon light, as the sun slips toward the horizon; it makes a warm and appetizing shade for an elegant dining room.

Pale, buttery yellow walls in a living or dining space make a wonderful backdrop for colorful painted furnishings and accessories; cobalt blue or turkey red in particular stand out against this setting. A grouping of celadon green pitchers or vases will also catch the eye when surrounded by light yellow.

Soft-toned yellow walls—the color of topaz—create an elegant backdrop for formal furnishings and rooms with generous proportions. Subdued yellows balance with the gleam of dark, polished wood, and enhance other mid-toned colors. Notice how blue-green trim elements in the dining room beyond this foyer take on added richness in the company of this gentle shade of yellow.

PAINT BOX

Using White with Pastels

WHEN CREATING A SOFT, PASTEL ROOM, TAKE CARE NOT TO OVERWHELM ITS COLORFUL ATTRIBUTES WITH TOO MUCH BRIGHT WHITE. USE MORE SUBTLE TONES OF WHITE IN THE COMPANY OF PALE TINTS, SO THAT THE PASTEL SURROUNDINGS LOOK DELICATE, RATHER THAN WATERED-DOWN.

SUBTLE TINTS OF YELLOW, SUCH AS PRIMROSE OR VANILLA CREAM, CREATE GENTLE SURROUNDINGS IN A BATH OR POWDER ROOM, WHERE A RESTFUL FEELING AND FLATTERING COLORS ARE IMPORTANT. WHITE FIXTURES WITH A VINTAGE LOOK, AND WHITE TILES WITH DECORATIVE PATTERNS CREATED WITH TINY BLACK OR COBALT BLUE TILES, COMPLETE A SOPHISTICATED AND COMFORTABLE SCHEME PAIRED WITH PALE YELLOW WALLS.

Pale yellow walls with vintage fixtures give this bath a refined, soft look. Mosaic detailing along the edges of the white tile and porcelain and brass accessories enhance the polished, period atmosphere.

Achieving the spicy look of curry requires two or more layers of toned-down yellow, with a darker, yellow-ocher glaze ragged over a smooth coat in a lighter hue. This luxurious room looks warm and mysterious using a complementary palette of yellows and deep violets. The ceiling border is an intricate relief pattern of vines and leaves, picked out in the lighter yellow to create an elegant and subtle harmony with the walls.

applying spicy shades of yellow

Mustard, saffron, and curry lend a snap to many ethnic dishes, and the deeper shades of yellow to which these spices give their names set a country mood when used on walls or trim. Mustard details for doors, windows, and perhaps a simple stenciled border along a wall's ceiling edge, define a room's dimensions when walls are painted in deep green, blue or red. Pick up this trim color with decorative pillows, lampshades, or nubby woven rugs for a warm, informal look.

Spicy yellow on the wall works like many deep-toned shades. It is enclosing and comforting, and a great foil for brilliant colors and sparkling accents. Chinese red or black lacquer furniture and deep, soft-cushioned seating in dark-bright hues – sapphire or emerald – create an indulgent, opulent ambience for a den or sitting room, when paired with walls rag-rolled in the lush yellow of saffron.

using yellow with metallic accents

Yellow has an illuminating effect in formal rooms, and marries well with elegant gilding and luxurious appointments. Ironically, decorating dictums in earlier centuries cautioned against using yellow in the company of gilt or gold metal, and many historic rooms show yellow walls with silver gilt framed art. Achieve a modern take on this archival scheme, and pair yellow walls with silver metallic furniture and fixtures for a sharp, contemporary blending of light and shine.

Yellow glazes can be mixed with metallic gold powders to create a shimmering effect over a lighter base coat. A sponged layer of this mixture is dazzling in a small dressing room or powder room, giving the space an air of regal elegance.

Gilded frames glamorize art and prints, and gilded details will do the same in formally furnished rooms. Moldings and trim can easily be detailed by brushing on gold metallic paint. If a room lacks such architectural ornament, it can be applied by stenciling a simple gold motif, such as a Greek key or egg-and-dart pattern around the ceiling edge. Similar decorative details can enhance a simply painted mantel; mask a narrow stripe around its perimeter and brush in a gold edge.

Use gold accents to enliven rooms painted in dark colors. Forest green, deep plum, rich brown, navy blue – these and most saturated colors are enriched with light-reflecting touches of gold. Create a stenciled border using gold and a contrasting accent color at ceiling or wainscot height. If paneling or doors have been painted in a dark color, pick out the details – the molding around wainscoting, the edges of door panels – in gold paint. In a vintage room from the gilded ages of the past – Georgian, Empire, or Victorian – applied architectural ornaments in rooms can be highlighted in gold for an authentic period look. Apply gold in proportion to a room's degree of luxury; embellished and tasseled swags, velvets, and taffetas can balance quantities of gilt more successfully than more modest fabrics, or highly patterned room furnishings. To get the right balance when painting trim, paint one detail at a time: one linear strip of molding, or one band of plaster trim around a ceiling fixture. It is always easier to add gilded details than it is to remove them.

Painting with Green

GREEN IS THE MAGICAL CHANNEL BETWEEN THE SUN AND THE EARTH AND ALL OF LIFE THAT IS

NOURISHED BY THESE ELEMENTS. Rare indeed are the flowers and fruit that do not bloom or

ripen against the backdrop of the many shades and tints of this life-sustaining hue. It is nature's

neutral, and those who love green discover that it has the same wonderful, mystical power

in the home.

Light Pistachio	Celery Ice	Limelight

① PALE AND YELLOW GREENS

Absolute Green	Summer Basket Green	Meadowlands Green

② MIDTONE GREENS

Ming Jade	Emerald Isle	Vine Green

③ DEEP GREENS

Peppermint Leaf	Fresh Scent Green	Hummingbird Green

④ JEWEL GREENS

The pleasing, airy atmosphere created by large windows and expansive views is enhanced by a kitchen design that brings outdoors in. Soft green walls and pale wood cabinetry, floors, and furnishings have a comfortable, natural feel, making this room a most relaxing space for cooking and gathering.

*The complementary relationship
of red and green extends to
all the tints and shades of each
hue. Here, coral-red walls are
subdued using two tones of blue-
green trim and decorative accents;
the palette is softened by the
balancing act performed by colors
at opposite ends of the spectrum.*

Almost any selection of colors can assert themselves in green surroundings. Positioned in the center of the spectrum, green can harmonize or complement any one of the other colors with ease. Think of a summer field, full of yellow, violet, blue, pink and red flowers; each can show off its vivid hue against the background of green leaves and stems. In this same fashion, green becomes a harmonizing base coat for other color combinations used in broken color treatments. And just as the many hues of green in forest and meadow can comfortably coexist and please the eye, so too can layers of different tints or shades of green create a monochromatic and appealing finish on walls. Versatile and comfortable, green creates harmony, unity, and vitality in room settings.

Just as other complementary schemes contain the element of surprising harmony – blue and orange, yellow and violet – the potential of a red and green pairing goes well beyond its use as a traditional Christmas palette. While pure red and intense green may make a team too energetic for most spaces, using these two colors in light- or dark-toned combinations creates palettes suitable for a variety of décors. Light green trim paired with coral red walls makes an elegant surround for light framed, painted furnishings. Rough walls color-washed in red and trimmed with green have a warm, country feel. The reverse palette – green walls with red trim – looks rich and formal with such furnishings as a red-based Oriental rug, and deep-cushioned upholstery that uses either red or green as a major fabric color. This setting can also set off and enhance shining lacquered tables and chairs, with green assuming its role as an enhancer and harmonizer of color and texture.

painting with pale green

Pastel green – think of pistachios, celery stalks, or the tiniest hint of new growth emerging from the ground – has enjoyed a resurgence in the home palette not seen since the Art Deco era of the 1930s. This fresh hue creates a feeling of serenity and a clean, healthy appearance in rooms where it is applied. Not surprisingly, pale green finds its way to bedrooms, baths, and other spaces where tranquility rules. Artfully colorwashed or sponged on walls, or painted in a satiny smooth coat, pale green brings a springlike quality to interiors that delights the eye and calms the beholder.

A collection of objects in pure, primary hues blends harmoniously before a background of soft green, revealing this color's amazing capacity to unify and enhance the clarity of objects it surrounds. Green is a spectral color that can easily function as a neutral in rooms.

applying yellow green

An interesting adjunct to soft pastel green is its more yellow neighbor on the color wheel: chartreuse. While this intense green hue has enjoyed popularity as a fashion color – albeit briefly – in several recent decades, its ability to combine cheerfully with expanses of white, with natural wood, and with touches of strong colors such as turquoise make it worth consideration for painting rooms. The bit of yellow in this hue can bring a lovely touch of light to rooms that could use more sunshine; mitigating its acidity with white and bright blue creates a pleasing and lively palette that will withstand the fickle whims of fashion.

using midtone greens

Pure bright green, toned down with gray and touches of blue or yellow, creates a variety of soft shades that effect a tranquil atmosphere in rooms. Use these hues to stencil leaves or vines in an appealing pattern along wall perimeters. To apply a Monet-like impression of flowers blooming in fields, sponge a layer of soft green glaze on walls,

Walls colorwashed to achieve the tang of lime juice provide lively counterpoint to the white fittings in this bath. Yellow-greens can be especially effective in small spaces; mitigate their sharpness with accents of pure bright hues for balance. In this room, turquoise window trim is a bright detail in the right proportion to harmonize the expanses of white and chartreuse.

Gray-green provides handsome surroundings when applied in a smooth coating to walls; its gentle tone creates a muted backdrop for wall-hung collections, and is particularly suited for walls displaying detailed, patterned objects. The beauty of decorated plates and platters, which would be hidden in a china cabinet, comes to life when arranged on a soft green wall.

Gray-green, along with many subdued shades of blue-green, enhance many vintage interiors. Not only does this color range harmonize with furnishings and accessories of the Arts and Crafts period at the turn of the twentieth century, gray-green is also a classical choice, one of the hues in the Wedgwood spectrum of the eighteenth century. Smooth gray-green walls make a flattering environment for a grouping of Mission-style furniture, and at the same time, this wall color will harmonize with the delicate carvings and curves of Federal and Georgian furnishings.

painting with deep green

The lush, dark colors of an evergreen forest or the leaves of holly and ivy make dramatic statements in the home. Sitting rooms and hallways hung with paintings in gilt frames look elegant and dramatic with shiny, deep green walls outlined with glossy white trim. Fill this setting with luxurious appointments—burgundy red velvets, shining dark wood furniture, and sparkling crystal—and feel enveloped in comfort and ease.

A vintage treatment pairs dark green walls in a flat finish with ivory or taupe trim, a somewhat muted combination that combines gently with country antiques—painted furniture, folk art, old patchwork quilts in many calico colors. Reverse the combination—taupe walls with spruce green trim—as a background for a neutral scheme accented with touches of blue or red in chair cushions, pillows, or window valances.

Using a soft gray-green for dining room walls helps reveal the intricate details of a display of vintage Staffordshire dinnerware. The same shade, applied to the frames and moldings of patio doors, creates a seamless passageway, permitting garden greenery to visually enhance the interior as well as the patio.

Dark green walls in the bathroom, with white or natural wood trim and fittings, create a feeling of warm repose – a perfect environment for a soak in the tub. Since this is a setting for letting the imagination roam free, give the bath a rustic feeling. Wash raw umber over tan for the look of rough plaster walls, then stencil or hand-paint trailing dark green vines around door and window moldings. The bath becomes a lovely private grotto, and a relaxing retreat.

working with jewel-tone green

Emerald and turquoise are gems prized for their brilliance, and they illuminate rooms with an inner light. A translucent emerald glaze ragged over a lighter green smooth coating can make a sitting room or inner hallway glow; add another layer of clear glaze combined with metallic powder for a lustrous, sparkling treatment that needs no further adornment.

Turquoise – sometimes seen as a shade of green-blue, at others as a blue-green – can add accents of intense color to rooms with a neutral palette. It balances sharp yellows, oranges, and reds, giving rooms a Southwestern feel when used with this color range. Using turquoise full strength on a wall makes a powerful color statement, an intense glow that can be softened with furnishings of rustic light wood, or bright white trim and moldings. Like walls in other strong hues, turquoise harmonizes with large pieces of wood furniture with a distressed or hand-hewn look, primitive objects, and the strong sunlight of southern latitudes.

Dark green walls can be lively and warm, and provide a strong but gentle field for objects placed before them. Details of sculpture and gilding are sharpened; this hallway scene shows how green can ease the eye like a soft neutral shade. Also note how pleasing the pairing dark green makes with the blue walls and ceiling in the dining room beyond.

PAINT BOX

Protecting Broken Color Finishes

PROTECT BROKEN COLOR FINISHES IN THE BATH, AND IN OTHER ROOMS WHERE HANDS MAY TOUCH WALLS OR MOISTURE CAUSE DAMAGE. APPLY A CLEAR SEALER SUCH AS POLYURETHANE, WHICH IS AVAILABLE IN ALL GLOSS LEVELS. CHECK WITH THE PAINT DEALER TO MAKE SURE THE SEALER WILL ADHERE TO THE CHOSEN PAINT SURFACE.

As a member of the green family, even high-intensity turquoise can function as background to collections of objects. A grouping of botanicals, suspended by visible lines, creates a high-impact impression when mounted over the turquoise ground. In this room, the rustic wood mantel and white trim balance turquoise's color power.

Painting with Violet

VIOLET SPEAKS OF MYSTERY AND POWER AND HAS BEEN APPROPRIATED THROUGH THE AGES BY SORCERERS AND ROYALTY ALIKE. A SECONDARY HUE MIXED FROM PRIMARY RED AND BLUE, THIS NEAT BALANCE BETWEEN WARM AND COOL HAS RECENTLY BEGUN TO EARN A MORE IMPORTANT PLACE IN THE MODERN HOME PALETTE. Victorians loved violet and used it everywhere, from the exteriors of their "painted lady" villas to dining rooms and parlors. While it has often been chosen for feminine bedrooms and pampering baths, this color can create dramatic and harmonious schemes throughout the home in living rooms, dining rooms, and even kitchens.

Everyone knows the traditional connection between lavender and lace, but violet functions equally well as a pleasing backdrop for modern, sculptural furnishings. Mid-tone violet has the intensity of warm gray, so that it creates a feeling of comfort and ease amid the sharp geometric planes and shiny finishes of contemporary spaces.

A pastel scheme lends elegance to this contemporary guest room; the gentlest touch of violet enhances this room's contemplative quality. Pale violet, teamed with white trim and spare black-lacquered accessories, plays the role of a meditative neutral, softening the room's angles and contributing to an atmosphere of restful quiet.

Lavender Mist	Misty Lilac	Whisper Violet	① SOFT VIOLET
Purple Hyacinth	Crocus Petal Purple	California Lilac	② NATURAL VIOLET
Twilight Magenta	Amethyst Cream	Enchanted	③ CONTEMPORARY VIOLET
Gentle Violet	Dark Lilac	Grape Gum	④ DEEP PURPLE

Soft violet effects a warming environment for this dining room, bringing out the rich glow of sculptural wood table and chairs, and dramatically framing the contemporary painting.

In a monochromatic scheme, a mixture of tints and shades of violet can be as lovely and fresh as a spring garden full of pansies, violets, lilacs, and tulips. This combination, applied in a broken color effect, lends a soft, contemplative quality to a spa bathroom or powder room, and creates a comfortable setting in a guest room.

A fine-arts approach pairs violet with its complement – yellow – a pleasing combination one can observe in nature in nearly every season: violet and daffodil, morning glory and primrose, aster and goldenrod, deep purple ash leaves and golden maples. Use this team in a dining room or a living room furnished with lots of light-stained wood. Use violet as the wall color with pale buttery trim, or reverse the combination, painting walls yellow with glossy violet trim. The most comfortable duets use the two colors at similar values.

Because yellow and violet have this symbiotic relationship, consider violet walls for a collection of paintings, prints, or photographs in gilded frames, which will glow in this juxtaposition.

Since violet's place in the spectrum falls between red and blue, either of these hues will work with it in a related scheme, used as trim or accent colors, as secondary colors for adjacent walls, floors or ceilings, or as partners in a broken color wall finish. On a wall, sponging clear glazing liquid colored with red or blue over a violet-sponged layer can create the luminous effect of a summer bouquet seen through sheer curtains.

using soft violet

A few moments after the sun sets, the sky streaks with pastels in a rainbow of colors. Among these hues are clouds tinted an elegant lavender. This inspiring combination sets the tone for a lovely broken color wall finish, using a smooth background of pale blue or pink, and sunset clouds of pale lavender pounced over the base with a sponge or a rolled rag. Consider such a finish for a sitting room or bedroom, a soft effect for a cozy space that inspires reflection. Or use a pale violet for a smooth painted wall, and one other pastel – pale pink, peach, and a whitened sky blue – as a trim color.

painting with natural violet hues

Violet works in amiable partnership with a variety of colors, and one of the most natural combinations blends it with green. A colorwash of violet over a white or pale gray base, trimmed with stenciled leaves or painted green moldings or wainscoting, brings a spring or summer palette indoors. For an effect that is soft, yet sophisticated, combine such a scheme with white painted furniture in a dining room or white upholstery in a living room.

Violet walls and a lush outdoor landscape soften the formality of gleaming dark wood furnishings in a bedroom lit by foliage-filtered natural light. The lilac paint treatment and bed covers are not overly sweet; using a rug and upholstery in white, and adding judicious touches of a related color – in this case a berry red – give the room an elegant balance.

Using an undercoat of white and a reverse stenciling technique—applying star shapes and a scalloped template along the ceiling—the dusky violet colorwash creates a nursery with a delightfully dreamy wall pattern. The effect creates a serene environment for the newest member of the family.

The tiny, pale purple florets of the lilac flower seem to shimmer amid its silvery-green foliage and the tan bark of its branches. Think of this combination in a room setting – pale or pickled wood furniture, with upholstery in one of the gray-greens. Walls might be a smooth, single pale purple tint or a sponged combination of several violet tints and shades; sponge randomly over the violet background with silvery green for an abstract, impressionist representation of these lovely, fragrant blooms.

Bedrooms, often placed in the floor plan at the rear of the house, frequently offer the most natural views: toward a backyard garden, fields or woods, or distant hills. Windows surrounded by walls painted violet help bring the outdoors in, as greenery is more noticeable in violet's company. The effect is soft and serene, just the right note for rooms set aside for dreams and rest.

using purple accents

Violet is a favorite children's color, as the popularity of certain purple dinosaurs will attest. With its regal connotations, violet can certainly please a resident young princess, and also takes its place in the playroom, used in its brightest tints along with the primary hues. Think about bright, shiny violet as a trim color in a child's room, for closet doors, window shutters, and wood furniture. While such an accent scheme works well with white walls, consider using it as trim when walls are a related color, sponged either in red or in blue. Or apply yellow – violet's complement – in a pale tint on the walls, using purple as a trim color and white for furniture and curtains to softly subdue the bright contrast.

Shades of plum have long been used in country schemes, and add to the coziness and warmth of spaces used for eating and gathering. Restore an old kitchen by painting wood cabinetry in a rich plum; detail moldings and pulls with a brighter violet hue to add contemporary flair.

Violet also works well in the company of soft gray, used as a trim color, or painted on a single wall to create a focal point. Broken color effects using violet as the top color have a pleasant warmth and softness when applied over a gray ground.

using violet in contemporary settings

The word purple sometimes conjures a vision of antiques, lacy antimacassars, maiden aunts, and bone china teacups. Yet this hue has begun to find its way into many modern and even minimalist interiors. A cool interior of flat, unadorned planes gathers warmth and definition with color, and lavender is sufficiently understated to work with modernist patterns of studied simplicity.

To create an effect of shadow play in an otherwise sun-struck space, use lavender on the vertical planes of a room in a single direction – all walls facing east, for example – while other walls are painted white or beige. Such a scheme provides contrast and spatial definition in a room without moldings or other architectural details.

Another common feature of contemporary homes, a high-ceilinged hallway, has a vertical volume that can make it feel cavernous. Painting walls in soft violet can humanize and soften such large-scale spaces.

PAINT BOX

OBTAIN THE EFFECT OF SOFTLY TINTED CLOUDS ON WALLS OR CEILING BY USING THE PARCHMENT BROKEN COLOR EFFECT DETAILED IN CHAPTER THREE OF THE FIRST SECTION OF THIS BOOK. THIS TREATMENT LOOKS FILMY AND ALMOST ETHEREAL, AS CONTRASTED WITH THE PUFFY CLOUDS THAT CAN BE ACHIEVED BY SPONGING ON A SKY-COLORED BASE.

Many contemporary kitchens have been outfitted with the latest sleek appliances, cloaked in brushed stainless steel for a clean, state-of-the-art appearance. And, just as violet makes a surprisingly good background for metallic finishes in other areas of the home, walls painted in a spring-fresh shade of hyacinth bring a space-age kitchen back to homey reality. Decidedly a fresh take on color in the kitchen, violet blends beautifully with the chrome, stainless, and nickel accoutrements that are now so popular in culinary design.

painting with deep purple

Lustrous eggplants, regal purple velvet, an amethyst brooch—all of these objects glow in the deepest shades of violet. Used on the walls of a cozy sitting room or library, these colors lend an air of intimacy and luxury. While flat-painted, deep purple walls duplicate the look of velvet or suede, using a shiny overcoat of glaze will give the same walls a glowing quality that reflects evening candlelight.

A room painted in deep purple is the perfect setting to use complementary yellow in its most luxurious form. Touches of gilt can be applied to moldings, and brass lamps, paintings with gold-leaf frames, and fabrics woven with golden thread sparkle in the company of violet walls. Think of jewel colors as possible accents for this extravagant scheme; fabrics, rugs, or accessories with hints of ruby, sapphire, or emerald complete the look.

Chrome and stainless steel fixtures, shelves, and equipment seem to glow more brightly in this violet-painted kitchen. The lovely, hyacinth background makes colored glass and fresh produce stand out in sharp relief. Violet seems to recede and blend with silvery objects, so while it is vibrant and fresh in a kitchen setting, it functions almost like a neutral hue in these surroundings.

PAINT BOX

ADD A BIT OF ARCHITECTURAL INTEREST TO PLAIN PAINTED CABINETS BY USING AN ACCENT COLOR NOT ONLY FOR CABINET PULLS, BUT ALSO TO CREATE THE ILLUSION OF A MOLDING WITH A PAINTED STRIPE NEAR THE EDGE OF CABINET DOOR PERIMETERS.

DO THIS WITH TWO LINES OF MASKING TAPE, LEAVING THE DESIRED STRIPE WIDTH AS A GAP BETWEEN THE TWO. TAKE CARE THAT THE LINES ARE STRAIGHT (MEASURE AND CHECK WITH A SPIRIT LEVEL) AND THE CORNERS ARE CRISP. BURNISH THE TAPE TO INSURE THAT EDGES ARE SMOOTH AND PAINT DOES NOT BLEED UNDERNEATH. WHEN PAINT IS DRY, REMOVE THE TAPE TO REVEAL THE STRIPE.

Deep purple, in the saturated
shade of an eggplant's skin,
creates a delightfully rich harmony with white in this vintage
living room. The dark walls cast
all the room's beautiful details—
the sheen of fabrics, the glow of
metallic frames and accessories,
the crispness of architectural
forms—in sharp relief.

Painting with Orange

ORANGE IS A SPRAK, A BURST OF ENERGY. IT EMBODIES A LIVELY FRESHESS, WHICH, LIKE THE TANGY FRUIT THAT BEARS ITS NAME, ADDS ZEST TO ANY ROOM IT DECORATES. As an advancing

color in the spectrum, organe may seem intimidating to use in any quantity in the home.

Applied in the right proportion and tone, however, its bright warmth provides excitement

in the decorative palette.

Incorporate orange in a related color scheme, using yellow and red, its neighbors on the

spectrum, to create a comfortable range for the eye. The total effect of all these advancing

colors can be softened by using white or beige for trim, fabric, or floor covering; the resulting

scheme is bright, but soft.

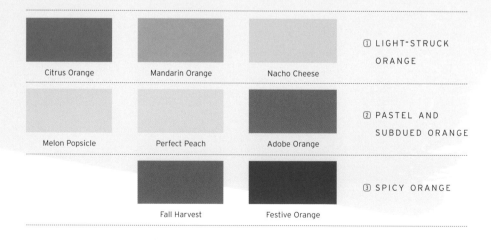

Citrus Orange   Mandarin Orange   Nacho Cheese

① LIGHT-STRUCK ORANGE

Melon Popsicle   Perfect Peach   Adobe Orange

② PASTEL AND SUBDUED ORANGE

Fall Harvest   Festive Orange

③ SPICY ORANGE

Bright orange can override almost any other color, but when it is colorwashed over a creamy base, it becomes translucent and soft, as if seen through a veil, or sheer curtains. This sitting room, rendered with an orange glaze over an ivory base, has the light, shimmering look of sorbet.

Walls painted in the warm shade evocative of ripe persimmons create a welcoming space in an entry foyer or home office. This cheerful color is a soft complement to painted wood; the blue desk looks rich and vibrant in this setting. See how the landscape in the gilded frame seems to acquire greater depth with the backdrop of midtoned orange.

Restrain the vivacious brightness of orange using any one of the broken color techniques. Rag rolling, sponging, or dragging orange over a pale ground adds the spark without too much flame. Consider using orange mixed with a clear glaze to further increase its transparency. Walls given this treatment will surely brighten a dark, windowless nook or hallway.

Apply bright orange paint, full-strength, to effectively focus the eye anywhere it is used. Covering one wall, a door, a window shutter, or a fireplace surround, orange will draw attention to any architectural detail. To make such a statement easier on the eye, use furnishings or accessories in shades of complementary blue or a rich, very dark green.

using light-struck orange

Just as a glass of orange juice becomes the sparkling centerpiece of a breakfast tray, walls washed with orange color illuminate a room that is bathed in morning light. Orange in its lighter tints is a refreshing color to wake up to, particularly if a gentle touch is used with furnishings. Pair orange-painted walls with light woods and floor coverings, pale textiles, and wall and window trim in white touched slightly with yellow, and the result is a sunny, harmonious atmosphere even when the day dawns cloudy. To further soften the attention-getting aspect of this hue, paint walls using orange tinted up with white or toned down with gray (or with its complement, blue) to make a room softer, easier on the eye.

painting with pastel orange

The pale orange pulp of a cantaloupe suggests a soft, pastel palette good for sunny climates, or for warming up rooms in cooler places. The addition of light tints of orange to a palette that contains such colors as icy blue or pale honeydew green provides a temperature adjustment equal to the sun's rays; an equivalent light tint of yellow might fade out in a brightly lit room, but pastel orange holds its own. In a houseful of rooms washed with pastels, pale melon trim throughout provides a unifying stroke of warm color to insure that the overall effect is lively, rather than faded.

Peach-painted rooms flatter many skin tones; peach is a glowing tint of orange that has a bit of red in it. Use it in bedrooms, powder rooms, even dining rooms, as orange—the color of so many fruits—is logically considered an appetite stimulant.

SOFT ORANGE EFFECTS

Late season orange fruits have a toned-down hue associated with the harvest, and a sense of warmth and coziness. Rich but subdued, these shades of festive gourds and mouth-puckering fruit enliven a space without overwhelming it with brightness. Use one of these darker oranges in a foyer to make it inviting and comfortable. The orange midtones also make a particularly good backdrop for painted furnishings.

Peach walls flatter this room's assets; polished wood floors and furniture shimmer as part of a scheme that includes coordinating fabric in related colors on the chairs. A mirrored wall reflects the overall glowing effect, heightening the soft, complexion-enhancing tone of the walls and the rich formality of the furnishings. Creamy white trim is the finishing touch for this elegant space.

Multiple layers of orange glaze, going from pale to midtone, with a final coat mixed with copper pigment, effect a luscious, glowing treatment for dining room walls. Glossy red-orange painted trim and upholstery, and shining accents, including sculptural copper light sconces, complete a glamorous, stimulating environment.

PAINT BOX

Conceal Flaws with Terra-Cotta

TERRA-COTTA IS A GREAT COLOR FOR WALLS THAT ARE LESS-THAN-PERFECT. USE IT AS A WALL COLOR IN A MATTE FINISH, LIKE THE COLOR OF COUNTRY TILE AND CLAY FLOWERPOTS, TO CONCEAL MANY SMALL FLAWS IN AN EXPANSE OF WALL.

painting with subdued shades of orange

Paint a wall with a single coat of light yellow or pale tan; then wash it with one or more coats of orange-tinted glaze for an effect to simulate the broad, glowing evening sky of the American southwest. The bright sun of this hot desert climate invites strong color that will not fade out under its rays. Colorwashed walls, of true rough plaster or a treatment that simulates this look, are an ideal background for rustic furnishings, Native American pottery, desert landscapes, wrought iron sculptures and candlesticks.

The orange of flowerpots and floor tile is a soft color that harmonizes with many decorating styles. Terra-cotta, the Italian words for "baked earth," possesses a homey warmth that makes it a wonderful wall color for public rooms where people gather, such as kitchens, family rooms, and living rooms. Because it is such a subtle shade of orange, it can easily work with bright, contrasting colors, as well as many different shades of blue and green, and not overpower other decorating elements. Rather than a strong statement, terra-cotta makes a wonderful background to the room's décor and activity.

Amber—a jewel-like substance, which catches light and seems to glow from within, inspires a shimmering wall color. Paint a base coat of slightly orange-beige, washed or rag-rolled with an amber-shaded glaze, to provide a luminous treatment. This color blends particularly well with the earthy tones of furnishings and decorations of the early twentieth century Arts and Crafts movement. Copper, verdigris, and hammered bronze—metals used for lamps and hardware in this era—look rich and warm in amber surroundings.

PAINT BOX

Keeping Light Patterns in Mind

KEEP IN MIND THAT LOCAL NATURAL LIGHT PATTERNS ALTER THE WAY COLOR APPEARS IN A DESIGN SCHEME. THOSE WHO LOVE SOUTHWESTERN COLORS AND STYLE, BUT LIVE IN NORTHERN LATITUDES, SHOULD CONSIDER USING COLORS IN A SLIGHTLY MORE TONED-DOWN PALETTE. ADVANCING HUES THAT HAVE A "HOT" APPEARANCE—RED, ORANGE, BRIGHT YELLOW—SHOULD BE TESTED IN THE HOME ENVIRONMENT USING A LARGE SAMPLE OF THE FINISHED EFFECT.

Terra-cotta walls function as a soft backdrop for many styles of furnishings. While it is often associated with rustic environments and country pottery, here the color works to warm effect with an eclectic grouping of furniture and accessories. Bright red—the small model cars on the lower shelf of the side table, and the background of the period print—works well with terra-cotta, as do other intense primary hues and bright orange. This subdued orange background enhances blue-green furnishings, such as the wicker chair and pottery pitcher.

Walls that glow are the effect of multiple layers of related colors that imitate light shining through amber beads. Wash a darker orange over a creamy base coat with a slight tint of yellow-orange to produce this luminous quality, which enhances many earth-toned objects and furnishings. Here, the walls make an appropriate vintage statement; amber was popular in the Arts and Crafts period, when such objects as the green art pottery and angular oak furniture heralded a break with highly-decorated Victorian formality.

spicy orange effects

Cinnamon, nutmeg, allspice, and cumin are pungent spices in subtle shades of orangey brown; their colors warm up the surroundings in any home, but blend especially well with country-style furnishings and natural materials. Subtle color variations among these spices create a pleasing palette for adjoining rooms, or a whole house.

The deepest tones of orange have a quiet, but intense warmth. These spicy, seemingly brown, colors work well in country interiors because of their earthy quality. Like all dark shades, spicy hues will glow more brightly when juxtaposed with white or cream-colored trim; this contrast will also make the space more formal, just as white collar and cuffs dress up the sports jacket.

using the metallic sheen of orange

Consider how a rack of hanging copper pots, or a wall covered with a display of copper molds can enhance a kitchen. Then consider the effect of a coppery orange wall: a yellow-orange base, sponged or washed with a coppery metallic tinted glaze. This shimmering wall could be the ideal place for a collection of kitchen wares; a grouping of colorful plates, a collection of water pitchers lined up on a plate rail, or an assortment of trivets would all stand out on such a glowing backdrop.

PAINT BOX

Consider Your Surroundings

ALWAYS CONSIDER THE VIEW THROUGH
A DOORWAY IN A DECORATING PLAN, AS
COLOR, LIGHT, AND FURNISHINGS IN
ONE ROOM SHOULD HARMONIZE WITH
WHATEVER CAN BE SEEN OF ADJACENT
SPACES. WHEN TESTING COLOR SAMPLES
FOR THEIR APPEARANCE NEXT TO A
ROOM'S FURNISHINGS AND IN VARYING
LIGHTS AT DIFFERENT TIMES OF DAY, BE
SURE TO PLACE THE SAMPLES IN DOOR-
WAYS LEADING TO ADJACENT ROOMS
FOR A COLOR JUXTAPOSITION THAT IS
PLEASING TO THE EYE.

*Cinnamon walls and pale
orange-brown clay floor tiles
make a monochromatic background for an array of country
furnishings; crisp white trim
gives this sitting room a touch
of formality. Seen through the
doorway, walls painted with a
lighter tint suggest a different
spice, blending well with the
front room and creating a sense
of visual harmony.*

Painting with Neutrals

TO UNDERSTAND THE ROLE OF NEUTRAL COLORS, CONSIDER A TRADITIONAL WINTER LANDSCAPE

IN A TEMPERATE CLIMATE: SNOW, BARE TREES, FRAGMENTS OF DRIED GRASS, GRAY BOULDERS,

AND LEAFLESS SHRUBS STICKING OUT FROM THE ICY TERRAIN ON AN OVERCAST DAY.

Without an impression of strong color, other visual qualities become apparent; details of form

and texture seem more pronounced. This is the power of a neutral palette, and the reason it

remains an ever-popular strategy for painting rooms.

Black and white and all tones of gray in between, plus the lighter side of the brown family,

constitute those hues that are considered neutral. Yet this label does not mean that using

neutral paints in rooms will result in drab or unexciting spaces. Every paint color makes a

statement, and these shades are no exception. Anyone who has seen one knows the vitality

of a successful black-and-white room, or the enveloping comfort of an all-beige room full of

interesting shapes and textures.

Soft, subtle colors, such as the pale gray-beige used on bedroom walls, act as harmonizing backgrounds for many different neutral tones. The patina of old wood, subtly gilded objects, and fabrics in muted beiges and whites combine in a haven for tranquility and rest.

① SOFT NEUTRALS

Frosted Café	Kahlua And Cream	Butter Pecan

② NEUTRALS THAT MIMIC NATURAL MATERALS

November Skies	Wolf Gray	Wisp Of Mauve

③ BEIGE, BROWN, AND TAN

Big Bend Beige	Sandlot Gray	Santa Fe Tan

One of the most exciting aspects of a neutral palette is its broad flexibility: myriad combinations of whites, grays, beiges, and blacks work together harmoniously. Thus, pairs, triads, or quartets of neutral shades can be ideal for painting walls in broken color effects. A creamy ivory wall with a dragged or combed overcoat in a subtly darker shade of beige or gray creates a hint of pattern and texture in a room with many soft and smooth fabrics and surfaces. Walls with a pale undercoat can also be taped off in a large grid, the squares softly delineated by hand-rubbing beige or tan paint next to the taped areas with a soft rag. When the tape is removed, the painted effect creates an illusion of stone blocks—a lovely backdrop for classical, light-colored furnishings.

When a smooth coat of neutral color paint is used for walls and trim, a successful monochromatic scheme can be built by applying similar values of the same color for upholstery, floors, and most other furnishings. Then, punch up the drama of the scheme with fully saturated details. Use deep brown details—pillows, picture frames, candlesticks—with beiges and tans. Accessorize all-gray schemes with black-lacquered side tables and black-painted baskets. Craft an all-over white scheme, then add one other color, using a neutral such as straw or taupe, or a single bright hue from the color wheel, for accessories such as lamps, throws, and pillows.

applying white paints

Every manufacturer's fan deck of colors contains a large section of whites—sometimes more than one hundred different shades and tints of this supposed non-color. Bright whites make a crisp contrast to almost any other color; often used as a standard treatment for ceilings, they make an adjacent color look more lively and true.

Creamy whites, with a touch of yellow, orange, or brown, have a softer appearance. They mimic warm afternoon light, creating a serene setting for reading and relaxing—a great palette for a library, bedroom, or office.

Using creamy whites in discernibly different sheens on the walls of a room is one way to achieve an interesting, yet subtle, patterned effect. For example, stripe a room with an ivory hue, using eggshell and satin sheens of the same shade. This creates a light, formal look of striped damask. For another elegant hint of pattern, apply subtle stenciled borders in classical motifs along the perimeters of a room using this same serene juxtaposition of gloss levels.

Picking out trim, molding, doors and windows in glossy, creamy white creates a somewhat aged appearance in rooms, especially when these details are paired with walls finished in vintage colors. Off-whites, pearl-whites, and putty tans have this historical connotation for many decorators and designers.

Walls painted white and complemented with matching slipcovered pieces create an atmosphere of peace and serenity. Against this soft backdrop, details of form and texture catch the eye, which can easily take in subtle features of the room's accessories: the patterns of the plates on the wall, the rustic surface of the sideboard, the elegant curved legs of the small tables near the couch.

Paint effects that resemble stone
evoke a feeling of classical
antiquity in a hallway, living
room, or any formal space.
Here, walls are painted to
resemble large blocks of limestone, rendered with a simple
technique of taping and ragging
off several layers of glaze
over a cream base. While this
marble mantel is the genuine
article, refer to Chapter Three
of Section One for painting
similar marble effects.

painting with soft, neutral tones

The gentle qualities of pale neutral colors lend themselves to painting linear or subtle geometric patterns. When used together, soft beiges, tans, whites, and grays will never clash. By vertically taping a white base coat, stripes of any pale neutral tint will energize a room and also provide an illusion of greater ceiling height.

Taping off sections of wall and painting them in a different soft, neutral shade artfully define a room's important features. Surround a large abstract canvas or a hall table with a painted rectangle or square of a neutral shade slightly darker than the base wall color. This subtle "framing" effect draws the eye to such focal points.

using neutral paints to mimic natural materials

Slate, marble, granite, and limestone are durable and beautiful natural materials that have become highly desirable for surfacing walls, floors, and countertops. Yet their distinctive – and expensive – good looks can be duplicated with a bit of practice. A wooden mantel or fireplace surround, artfully painted to suggest stone, creates an elegant focal point for a living or dining room.

Distinguish an entry hall by painting walls to resemble blocks of stone. Using a pale smooth base, tape off walls in squares that suggest quarried sections of limestone or sandstone. Then apply glazes in one or more soft shades that duplicate the chosen stone, rubbing along the taped borders to suggest the subtly shaded edges of cut stone.

PAINT BOX

Matching Natural Stone

TO CHOOSE A PALETTE FOR IMITATING NATURAL STONE, VISIT A DEALER WHO SPECIALIZES IN DECORATIVE STONE PRODUCTS AND OBTAIN A SAMPLE OF THE ACTUAL SURFACE TO BE DUPLICATED IN PAINT. REALLY LOOK AT ITS DETAIL, THE NUANCES OF SHADING, AND THE DIFFERENT NEUTRAL COLORS THAT COMPOSE ITS SURFACE.

THEN CHOOSE PAINT TO MATCH THE COLORS OF THE TRUE STONE. SOME LARGE PAINT STORES AND HOME CENTERS HAVE SPECIAL EQUIPMENT TO SCAN AND CUSTOM-MATCH COLOR FROM FABRIC SWATCHES AND OTHER SAMPLES. IT IS ALSO A GOOD IDEA TO PRACTICE STONE-PAINTING TECHNIQUE ON A SAMPLE BOARD BEFORE TRYING IT ON THE WALL.

Multiple textures increase the comforting appeal of this study, decorated in shades of brown from golden tan to milk chocolate. Rich caramel walls, velvet and leather furnishings, and crisp, white trim combine for a look that is both warm and elegant.

getting the look of granite

Imitate the rich, speckled surface of cut granite on bathroom walls or kitchen backsplashes with a simple sponging technique. Copy the colors of a favorite sample, which may have three or four different neutral shades: tan, white, gray, and black is one combination for a number of varieties from different quarries around the world. Use the lightest color in the granite sample for the base, then sponge in succession with glazes in the other colors, finishing with the darkest shade, allowing glazes to dry between colors. Depending upon the granite look desired, choose sponges in the pore size that will best replicate the sample.

using beige, brown, and tan

The colors of sand, bark, and wood provide a natural and relaxed harmony in rooms. Choosing one shade of the brown family for walls, and furnishing a space so enclosed with other tints and tones of this hue, creates an immediate sense of warmth and security. Because of their comforting, earthy quality, such palettes are often chosen for restful spaces: dens, family rooms, and spa bathrooms. The associations of libraries and spaces for work and reading with materials such as leather and tweed also make a case for painting walls in brown or tan.

Shiny glazed walls in deep chocolate, or warm textured or flat-finished walls in a soft fawn shade, make an elegant background for richly tactile furnishings in nubby fabrics, leathers, or velvets. Add a touch of formality with crisp, white trim. Or, soften and make the effect of brown or tan more rustic and countrified by colorwashing the chosen shade.

Matte black walls provide a
sophisticated backdrop for art
and antiquities, sharpening
the details of each object and
enhancing the impact of their
forms. The strategy of using
light-reflecting metal objects and
white trim lightens the atmosphere of the space so that the
broad black field looks bold,
but not somber.

Change Color to Change the Mood

WHEN TRYING TO DECIDE WHICH COLOR TO PAINT A ROOM, LOOK WITHIN BEFORE LOOKING AT PAINT CHIPS. ASK YOURSELF, WHAT ARE YOU GOING TO USE THE ROOM FOR? HOW DO YOU WANT TO FEEL WHEN YOU'RE THERE? How do you want your guests to feel? Do you want something elegant and reserved or something casual and relaxed? Do you want the room to make you think or to help you relax? In other words, pick the mood to help you pick the color. If you want the space to feel sophisticated, list your thoughts and find colors in magazines or on paint chips that elicit that sophisticated effect. Then, let these tones become your basic palette.

To conclude the color section of *Painting Rooms*, we offer the experience of designer Gregor Cann, who artfully refreshed one room of his house three times, with three different colors, in a single year. The opportunity to present such actual proof of the power of paint was simply irresistible, and we thank Gregor, photographer Eric Roth, and the publishers of the *Boston Globe*, for allowing us to share it on these pages.

orange-yellow paint for a burst of energy

To create a tropical break inside a wintry climate, paint a room with a brilliant and vigorous orange-yellow, such as safflower. This warm and alive color vibrates with energy, and people seem to noticeably perk up when they walk in the room.

To decorate with such a vibrant wall color, meet its boldness with similar bright accents. Use pillows in bold, bright colors to compete with the walls; paler shades would wimp out. Let the room be about fun and abandon—no need to be reserved. Consider larger and fewer pieces of furniture. Arrange furniture and accessories so that the lines are straightforward, gridlike, and clean.

blue for calm and tranquility

If you want a space to feel cool and kicked back, paint with blue — it lowers the energy and calms the pace. Blue lets your room or home exude a more come-as-you-are attitude, encouraging people to laugh and let go. Accent the room with a lot of whites to give it a crispness, an edge. Use a contrasting white for the furniture and artwork to let individual pieces stand out and take on greater importance. The lesson here: If you want to play up something, contrast it. The floor space is more defined in white. Conversely, the eye blends colors that are more alike, so each piece in the room has less definition. If you want to downplay that couch that needs to be recovered, paint the walls in a shade similar to the sofa fabric.

One blue note: The paler the shade of blue, the more tranquil and cooler, the effect. Blues can make a space seem chilly if you're not careful. Paint, with brighter blues — they are more vibrant and less cold.

PAINT BOX

REMEMBER THAT COLOR AFFECTS ITS NEIGHBORS. CONSIDER THE GOLD LEAF ON THE PICTURE FRAMES AND THE GOLD CHEST: THE GOLD LOSES ITS IMPORTANCE ON THE ORANGE WALLS, COMES FORWARD ON THE YELLOW-CREAM WALLS, AND IS IN YOUR FACE ON THE BLUE WALLS. SIMILARLY, THE SOFA STANDS OUT MORE IN THE BLUE ROOM THAN IT DOES IN THE OTHER TWO.

sophistication with yellow-beige

Create a room that feels poised and sophisticated by using a warm, yellowy beige. To accent and enhance this air of decorum, polish and display your fancy collections: cut glass, polished silver, orchids. Anything that says luxury and elegance. Be aware of the fine line between tasteful presentation and ostentatious display. If you want your home to be inviting but not pretentious, keep the elegance a little offhanded. Contrast glitz with some fundamental stuff — things that don't take machines and money to create, like fruit heaped in a crude clay bowl, firewood stacked on the floor, or roses crowded into a glazed pot.

PAINT BOX

CREATE DRAMA AND CONTROL CHAOS BY SPACING GROUPED ACCESSORIES EQUALLY, AS IN THE DISPLAYS OVER THE FIREPLACE AND THE COLLECTION OF CLAY POTS ON THE GLASS-TOPPED TABLE. THIS RULE OF STRENGTH IN NUMBERS IS ESPECIALLY IMPORTANT WHEN CONTRASTING ACCESSORIES AND ART WITH YOUR WALL COLOR. CLEAN LINES ARE EASIER ON THE EYE, SO DECIDE ON ONE CONCEPT AND STICK WITH IT.

BOX OF PAINT COLORS

Color inspiration comes from many sources. Some people love to leaf through magazines and books to find rooms they like, and take the pictures to the paint store to compare them with the paint cards. Others take cues from the natural world, looking at landscapes or flower gardens to help construct their interior palette. Many people just like to play with pure color, looking at chips and imagining the various hues on their walls. While the previous section of this book supplies many vignettes to study, and the text offers many suggestions of colors from nature, this book would not be truly finished without a supply of color samples to contemplate. Thanks to the generosity of Benjamin Moore & Co., the following pages present a sample of the vast spectrum of colors available from this respected company.

Of course, you may also want to visit your local dealer to inspect the hundreds of colors that could not be duplicated on these pages. Enjoy your search for the perfect color!

The colors used in this section refer to the Benjamin Moore® Color Preview System. These colors are printed and may vary from the actual paint colors. Please consult your Benjamin Moore & Co. dealer for the Benjamin Moore & Co corresponding color chips for accurate color. See the Resources (page 298) for contact information. If you would like to use paints from another range, the paint retailer of your choice will be able to advise you on the closest available match.

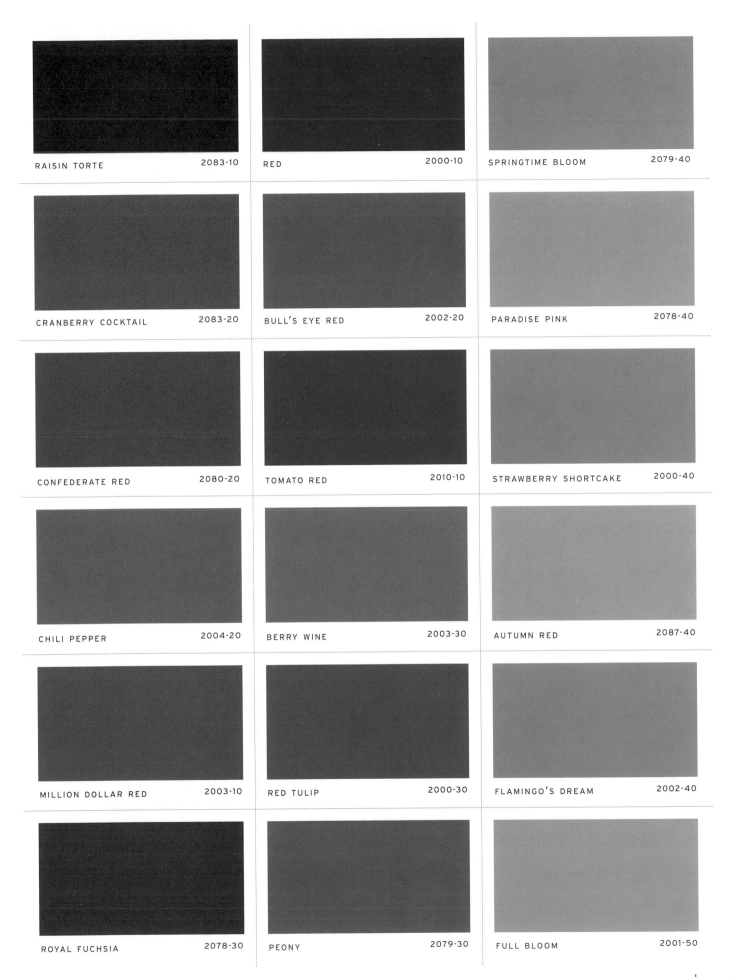

RAISIN TORTE 2083-10	RED 2000-10	SPRINGTIME BLOOM 2079-40
CRANBERRY COCKTAIL 2083-20	BULL'S EYE RED 2002-20	PARADISE PINK 2078-40
CONFEDERATE RED 2080-20	TOMATO RED 2010-10	STRAWBERRY SHORTCAKE 2000-40
CHILI PEPPER 2004-20	BERRY WINE 2003-30	AUTUMN RED 2087-40
MILLION DOLLAR RED 2003-10	RED TULIP 2000-30	FLAMINGO'S DREAM 2002-40
ROYAL FUCHSIA 2078-30	PEONY 2079-30	FULL BLOOM 2001-50

HYDRANGEA FLOWERS 2008-40	CANDY STRIPE 2079-70	MELON POPSICLE 2016-50
BLUSHING BRIDE 2086-50	MARMALADE 2016-40	PEACH CLOUD 2169-60
TICKLED PINK 2002-50	PEACHY KEEN 2014-40	ORANGE 2011-10
DELICATE ROSE 2008-50	PEACH SORBET 2015-40	FESTIVE ORANGE 2014-10
EARLY SUNRISE 2084-60	SPRINGTIME PEACH 2014-50	RUMBA ORANGE 2014-20
AZTEC LILY 2080-70	PERFECT PEACH 2167-50	ORANGE BURST 2015-20

TANGY ORANGE 2014-30	ORIOLE 2169-30	BUMBLE BEE YELLOW 2020-10
CALYPSO ORANGE 2015-30	ORANGE BLOSSOM 2168-30	NACHO CHEESE 2018-40
ADOBE ORANGE 2171-30	STARTLING ORANGE 2016-10	CITRUS BLAST 2018-30
FALL HARVEST 2168-10	CITRUS ORANGE 2016-20	LEMON SHINE 2020-20
ORANGE PARROT 2169-20	CARROT STICK 2016-30	SUNFLOWER 2019-30
PUMPKIN PIE 2167-20	MANDARIN ORANGE 2018-20	GOLDEN NUGGET 2019-20

YELLOW RAIN COAT 2020-40	BANANA YELLOW 2022-40	LEMON DROPS 2019-50
AMERICAN CHEESE 2019-40	LEMON FREEZE 2025-50	MORNING SUNSHINE 2018-50
LEMON 2021-20	YELLOW HIGHLIGHTER 2021-40	HAWTHORNE YELLOW HC-4
BABY CHICK 2023-20	BRIGHT YELLOW 2022-30	JASPER YELLOW 2024-50
SUN PORCH 2023-30	YOLK 2023-10	YELLOW LOTUS 2021-50
SUN KISSED YELLOW 2022-20	YELLOW FINCH 2024-40	LEMON MERINGUE 2023-60

MOONLIGHT 2020-60	PALE VISTA 2029-60	EMERALD ISLE 2039-20
LIGHT DAFFODIL 2027-60	LIGHT PISTACHIO 2034-60	JADE GREEN 2037-20
PALE STRAW 2021-70	CELERY ICE 2030-60	VINE GREEN 2034-20
SPRUCE GREEN 2035-50	ICED MINT 2030-70	PEPPERMINT LEAF 2033-20
LIMELIGHT 2025-40	ABSOLUTE GREEN 2043-10	TROPICAL SEAWEED GREEN 2030-20
FRESH CUT GRASS 2026-50	MING JADE 2043-20	FRESH SCENT GREEN 2033-30

GREEN GABLES 2041-30	CITRUS GREEN 2032-40	TWILIGHT BLUE 2067-30
HUMMINGBIRD GREEN 2042-30	STEM GREEN 2029-40	EVENING BLUE 2066-20
IGUANA GREEN 2028-10	TEQUILA LIME 2028-30	OL' BLUE EYES 2064-30
BRIGHT LIME 2025-10	EVE GREEN 2024-20	BLUEBERRY 2063-30
SUMMER BASKET GREEN 2040-40	BOLD BLUE 2064-10	SEAPORT BLUE 2060-30
MEADOWLANDS GREEN 2036-40	CHAMPION COBALT 2061-20	UTAH SKY 2065-40

SAILOR'S SEA BLUE 2063-40	BLUE LAKE 2053-40	BLUEBELLE 2064-60
CLEAREST OCEAN BLUE 2064-40	BLUE MARGUERITE 2063-50	WHITE SATIN 2067-70
BLUE LAPIS 2067-40	BLUE JEAN 2062-50	BLUE HYDRANGEA 2062-60
BLUE WAVE 2065-50	CARIBBEAN COAST 2065-60	BASHFUL BLUE 2065-70
COOL BLUE 2058-40	COSTA RICA BLUE 2064-50	HARBOR FOG 2062-70
COOL AQUA 2056-40	TURQUOISE POWDER 2057-50	PURPLE LACE 2068-60

LAVENDER MIST 2070-60	GRAPE GUM 2068-20	PASSION PLUM 2073-30
PALE IRIS 2073-60	DARK LILAC 2070-30	TWILIGHT MAGENTA 2074-30
LILY LAVENDER 2071-60	GENTLE VIOLET 2071-20	LILAC PINK 2074-40
PURPLE CREAM 2073-70	AUTUMN PURPLE 2073-20	PURPLE HYACINTH 2073-40
MISTY LILAC 2071-70	MYSTICAL GRAPE 2071-30	PURPLE EASTER EGG 2073-50
WHISPER VIOLET 2070-70	SCANDINAVIAN BLUE 2068-30	CROCUS PETAL PURPLE 2071-40

CALIFORNIA LILAC 2068-40	BLACK IRON 2120-20	MELLOWED IVORY 2149-50
SPRING PURPLE 2070-40	JET BLACK 2120-10	WHITE MARIGOLD 2149-60
VICTORIAN TRIM 2068-50	BABY SEAL BLACK 2119-30	ALPINE WHITE 2147-70
EXOTIC FUCHSIA 2074-50	BLACK BERRY 2119-20	EASTER LILY 2150-70
AMETHYST CREAM 2071-50	TOUCAN BLACK 2118-20	ADOBE WHITE 2166-70
ENCHANTED 2070-50	UNIVERSAL BLACK 2118-10	CANDLE WHITE 2164-70

PATRIOTIC WHITE 2135-70	SANDY WHITE 2148-50	EVENING DOVE 2128-30
ICE MIST 2123-70	YELLOW FREEZE 2020-70	WOLF GRAY 2127-40
ASPEN WHITE 2027-70	LION YELLOW 2158-60	EXCALIBUR GRAY 2118-50
MOONLIGHT WHITE 2143-60	IVORY TOWER 2157-70	NOVEMBER SKIES 2128-50
WOODLAND SNOW 2161-70	FINE CHINA 2156-70	BEACON GRAY 2128-60
SUGAR COOKIE 2160-70	TIMID WHITE 2148-60	SILVER CLOUD 2129-70

ROASTED COFFEE BEANS 2098-20	TAWNY 2161-20	CREAM 2159-60
SANTA FE TAN 2097-40	DUNMORE CREAM HC-29	SILKEN PINE 2144-50
PEBBLE STONE 2100-50	PEARL HARBOR 2165-50	CLOUD NINE 2144-60
SANDLOT GRAY 2107-50	BIG BEND BEIGE AC-37	ICED MAUVE 2115-50
WISP OF MAUVE 2098-60	KAHLUA AND CREAM 2161-60	TOUCH OF GRAY 2116-60
FROSTED CAFÉ 2098-70	BUTTER PECAN 2165-70	LATTE 2163-60

PAINTING
FURNITURE

painted *patterns*

BASICS OF
painting *furniture*

Painting is a great way to breathe new life into an old piece of furniture—or even to transform an ordinary newer piece of furniture into a focal point of a room. You may find an old end table in the attic or a piano bench at a yard sale. When you look at it, you're drawn to it, though you don't quite know why. You can see that even in a state of utter disrepair, the piece has an inherent charm. But how can you bring that out? This book provides several pattern and finish ideas that will inspire you to unlock the potential of any piece of furniture, from chairs to bureaus to tables to cabinets and more.

What you decide to paint is as important as how you decide to paint it. Obviously, a larger piece of furniture is going to make a stronger statement in a room than a smaller piece. Keep this in mind when you plan the piece. An elaborate and vibrant design painted on a large armoire is going to draw more attention than the same design on a small ladder-back chair. And conversely, a subtle stenciled pattern painted on a small, wall-mounted shelf may get lost, while the same pattern painted as a border treatment around the top of a dining room table will not.

The Essentials

Before you begin any painted furniture project, make sure you are prepared. There's nothing worse than having to stop a project in the middle to run out and get the right size brush or the furniture wax you need to do an aging technique. Here are some basic materials that are always good to have on hand:

- Several sharpened number-two pencils
- White chalk
- Tracing paper
- Sheets of oak tag or thin cardboard
- Smudge-resistant carbon paper
- Screwdriver to remove furniture hardware
- Sandpaper ranging from extra-fine to medium grit
- Painter and artist brushes in various sizes
- Exacto knife and spare blades
- Ruler and/or T-square
- Drop cloths
- Several clean cotton rags
- Empty jars of various sizes—including film canisters—for storing portions of paint mixtures you've created plus containers such as coffee cans for mixing paint
- Stirring sticks for mixing colors
- Painter's masking tape of varying widths

right for *the room*

When you paint a piece of furniture, there are many more elements to consider than just the "how to." A piece of painted furniture can have as much impact in a space as the color of the walls, the material used on the floors, or the window treatments. It can become the focal point of a room, changing the mood of a décor or even setting the tone for the rest of the interior design scheme to follow.

With that in mind, how to paint any particular piece of furniture should not be a decision you make lightly. Before you begin, step back and take a good look at the room where the piece will be housed. What is the room already conveying? Are there architectural elements to emphasize? How will the painted piece contrast with or complement other furnishings in the room? If the room doesn't already have a personality of its own, how can you give it one with the addition of a painted piece?

Taking inspiration from the existing décor is one way to decide what kind of project to undertake, but it's not the only way. Flip through interior design magazines and books. Do you have a favorite style that you always seem to stop on but are afraid to change your whole room with this look? Perhaps you've fallen in love with French country style, but you live in a contemporary home or a modern high-rise apartment building and you think that bringing that style in simply won't work against that background. Instead, satisfy your taste for French country style by distressing a small bench in your living room, or using an aging technique on a bureau. On the other hand, if you live in a nineteenth-century farmhouse, and you want to go full force on French country style, distressing the built-in cabinets in your family room or other prominent aspect of your home might just be the best way to start revamping your décor.

Think of how a small, round, bent-leg end table painted with a simple, English floral motif can infuse an entryway with charm. At one time an unnoticed drop point for keys and mail, the table now becomes a welcoming beacon into a tastefully decorated home. Consider how an old wooden chair, at one time an afterthought employed to fill an empty corner in the living room, can become a place where the guest of honor sits when painted in a rich, black lacquer with a gold-leaf motif. Imagine how a vibrantly painted striped shelf can brighten up an otherwise ordinary powder room—and still provide much-needed storage.

And isn't that what really sets a piece of painted furniture apart from other decorative aspects in a room, like wallpaper or art? By its very nature, furniture is for function. A chair is for sitting on. An armoire is for hiding clothes, and an entertainment center disguises a home office. A table is for dining, working, or gathering. But with a decorative paint treatment or a fresh coat of paint, these pieces become the art itself, elements that infuse a room with visual interest and that can ultimately become the focal point of any room.

PAIRING pattern & style

Choosing patterns to enhance your décor is, at heart, a personal process. While you may choose a pattern because you think it will set a particular style or mood in a room, if you don't intrinsically like the pattern, you're not going to be happy with the result. It may sound obvious, but if you are tempted to create a distinctively English country bedroom, and florals don't really do it for you, you'll be treading on dangerous ground if you include too many floral patterns in your design scheme. Do the research. Find out everything you can about a style and what goes into making that style before you get carried away with implementing it. When you learn more about English country style, you see that it's a rich style that relies on many different patterns—and in many cases, these patterns are all used together. So instead of florals, you might opt for a scheme that relies on plaids to get the point across, with small floral touches—perhaps in the form of a couple of tiny throw pillows for the bed, that are subtle enough to blend in with the décor but that are easily removed when you want a different look.

- Fine sandpaper
- Tack cloth
- Ruler
- Number-two pencil
- Chalk (optional)
- Masking tape
- Three paintbrushes: one 2-inch (5 cm) sponge brush for applying primer and base coat; one 1/4-inch (6 mm) round art brush for leaves; one 1/8-inch (3 mm) round liner brush for painting in vine and touch-ups
- One small can of water-based primer
- One small can of water-based, flat paint in pale sage green for basecoat
- One small can of water-based, flat paint in jasper green for vine
- One spray can satin-finish polyurethane

PAINTING SURFACE
An unfinished pine dresser

PATTERN
None required

COMPLETION TIME
Four hours
(including drying time)

Swedish colors are light and pastel, and that's the secret to creating the ultimate Swedish piece. In this project, we transformed a plain wooden table into a vanity by adding a simple apron to three sides. The piece is then finished with a pale mint–green color creates a delightful backdrop for a simple vine pattern.

swedish *lights*

Method

- This simple vine pattern requires only a few careful brush-strokes, but it's a good idea to practice your technique a few times before painting the finished piece.

- Try to paint the vine freehand, or mark a pattern lightly in pencil or chalk to follow.

- For a more elaborate effect, paint the vine motif on, or around, the table's legs.

starting *out*

Sand the table and remove any residue with tack cloth or slightly damp cloth. With the 2-inch (5 cm) brush, apply the first coat of primer. Allow top to dry thoroughly and apply the second coat.

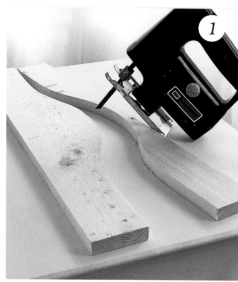

Step 1 Use a jigsaw to cut a wooden apron to fit around the back outside edge of the table. If you don't want to do this yourself, you may be able to have the wood cut for you at a home improvement store. Just bring a template.

Step 2 Secure the apron in place with strong wood glue. Drill through both layers to create a starter hole, then attach the apron firmly with wood screws.

With the 2-inch (5 cm) brush, apply two coats of primer to the table, allowing coats to dry thoroughly in between. With the 2-inch (5 cm) brush, paint the table completely in the light sage green base coat. Let dry thoroughly and apply a second coat.

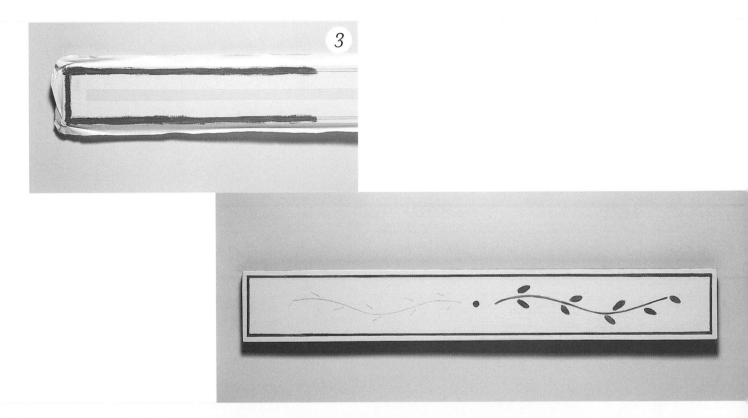

Step 3 With a ruler, measure in 1/2 inch (1 cm) from the edges of the front of table and mark with pencil or chalk. Mask off and paint border in jasper green with the 1/4 inch (1 cm) round artist's brush. Carefully remove masking tape upon completion. Allow paint to dry thoroughly before moving to the next step.

Step 4 If you are more comfortable doing so, draw in the vine pattern lightly in pencil or in chalk. With the 1/8-inch (6 mm) round liner brush, paint in vine pattern, following the photo on page 155.

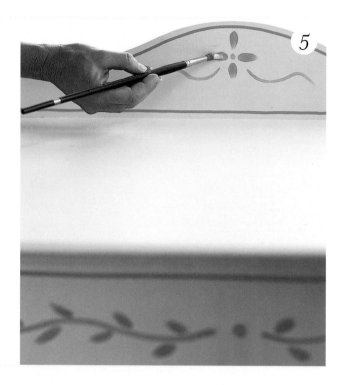

5

TIP

Flat-finish paint gives a soft effect perfect for Swedish design as well as Colonial-style rooms and the like. The main problem with flat-finish paint, however, is that it is difficult to clean and should only be used on items that don't get a lot of wear and tear. An alternative for a piece in a high-volume area is eggshell finish. It is barely reflective, so you can keep a subdued appearance, but is much easier to clean.

Step 5 Create a central floral motif as a centerpiece to two vines by painting four leaf shapes around a center dot. When the table is completely dry, spray with polyurethane top coat and let dry thoroughly.

variation

This variation mimics the original pattern, except that the pattern is more detailed and controlled. The antique white backdrop sets a delicate feel, perfect for a woman's vanity or dressing table. For a country look, change the colors. Try painting a blue leaf pattern over a beige background.

Method

This variation is performed in much the same way as the preceding project, but in this case, a tiny leaf shape was created, cut out, and traced around the vine, making for a more precise effect. First prime the table. Then paint two coats of the antique white basecoat. Once the basecoat has dried, create the border. Next, lightly draw in the vine with pencil or white chalk. Next, trace leaf shapes around the vine, following photo. Paint in vine using liner brush and leaves with round art brush.

Materials

- Fine sandpaper
- Tack cloth
- Ruler
- Number-two pencil
- Chalk (optional)
- Masking tape
- Three paint brushes: one 2-inch (5 cm) sponge brush for applying primer and base coat; one 1/4-inch (6 mm) round art brush for leaves; one 1/8-inch (3 mm) round liner brush for painting in vine and touch-ups
- One small can of water-based primer
- One small can of water-based, flat paint in antique white for basecoat
- One small can of water-based, flat paint in jasper green for vine
- One spray can satin-finish polyurethane

- Fine sandpaper
- Tack cloth
- A roll of 1-inch (3 cm) painter's masking tape
- Ruler
- Number-two pencil
- Two paintbrushes: one 2-inch (5 cm) sponge brush for base coat; one ½-inch (1 cm) sponge brush for stripes
- One small can of water-based primer
- One small can of latex-based paint, in pale pink
- One small can of latex-based paint, in medium pink
- One spray can satin-finish polyurethane

Brighten a plain white bathroom with a decorative shelf in warm pink tones. Or choose another soft color to coordinate with your bath linens or a cotton rug. You can adapt the pattern to highlight the silhouette of any simple wooden shelf.

pretty in *pink*

PAINTING SURFACE
A small pine bathroom shelf

PATTERN
None required

COMPLETION TIME
**Four hours
(including drying time)**

Method

- In this project, the lighter stripes are neatly nestled in the scallop cuts of the bottom portion of the shelf, but you can arrange them any way you like.

- How big should your stripes be? What works for your shelf will depend on how long it is. Rule of thumb: the dark pink stripes should be twice as wide as the pale pink ones. In this case, the pale pink stripes are 1 inch (3 cm) while the dark pink ones are 2 inches (5 cm) wide.

- Make sure you don't cover pencil marks with masking tape as you will most likely not be able to cover them up with the pink paint.

starting *out*

Sand down the shelf and remove any residue with the tack cloth. With the 2-inch (5 cm) brush, paint the shelf with two coats of primer, allowing coats to dry thoroughly in between.

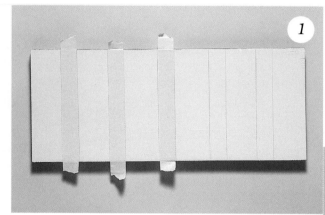

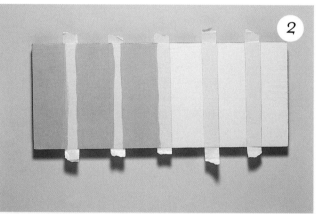

Step 1 Measure the width of the dark pink stripes across the shelf. Mark the width lightly in pencil or with chalk. Mask off the borders of the medium pink stripes.

Step 2 With the ½-inch (1 cm) brush, paint in dark pink stripes, being careful not to cover the masking tape. Carefully remove tape after painting. When the shelf is completely dry, spray with polyurethane top coat and let dry thoroughly.

variation

Starting out with a scalloped shelf? Why not highlight the shape of the piece by accenting the scallops with playful polka dots?

Materials and Method

Use the same basic materials for this project, substituting light spruce green for the base coat and white for the polka dots. You can use the tip of a pencil eraser to create the polka dots. Practice first on a sheet of paper to test out your design. You can also vary the size of the eraser for added interest. To start, prime the shelf and paint two coats of the light spruce green. When the base coat is thoroughly dry, dab the pencil eraser in the white paint and dot the shelf, following the photo to the right.

TIP

If you are not comfortable using a pencil eraser, you can always create a template for the smaller dots, or, depending on the size of your shelf, try using a dime. Larger polka dots can be created using a nickel or quarter.

PAINTING
OUTSIDE

Introduction

Since the publication of my book on interior wall paint color, people have been asking when I will write a book on exterior paint colors.

Choosing exterior colors is a much more daunting task, involving far more financial and aesthetic risk than choosing interior colors. The task baffles many people. To date, no reliable resources were available for guidance.

Paint color is the single most effective way to change the personality of your house and transform it to its best advantage. Paint color can change the appearance of your home's size, making it seem larger or smaller, taller or wider. It can highlight aspects of the architecture. Paint can make your house stand out from or blend into its surroundings, whichever you desire. To an undistinguished home, properly chosen paint color can add a new sense of design and style.

Color selection is not easy. Paint chips are small and houses are large. The simplest solution would be to find a house similar in style to your own that is painted in colors you love and ask the occupants what colors they used. If only it were that easy! Many of you don't know what color you want your house to be. Others know you want yellow, for instance, but don't know which specific yellow to choose from the thousands available.

> **Many who want to do what** will be considered in good taste are puzzled to know what colors to use, and how to direct their painter so as to give him a tolerably clear idea of what they want. —Ehrick Kensett Rossiter and Frank Ayers Wright, *Modern House Painting*, 1882

You don't want to make a paint color mistake on your house. It's far too costly. Using this book, you can rest assured you will choose the right colors. I show you everything you need to know, including optimum color coordination of the house, the trim, shutters, window boxes, and so on. Consideration is also given to flowers, shrubs, and walkways. You will have the exact paint color numbers in hand when you are ready to purchase paint. In addition, you will have all the information you need to ensure a lasting paint job. After all, you are protecting and preserving your largest investment from the elements. I answer your color questions—"What color should I paint the garage door?"—and technical questions—"What kind of surface preparation does my stucco home need before painting?" "How much should it cost to have my house painted?"

The following section comprises three parts. The first covers introductory material on choosing house paint colors, including step-by-step guidelines and information on the painting process itself. The main body of the text offers color recipes—ready-made color combinations for the exterior of the house.

This section is subdivided by color: red, orange, yellow, green, blue, violet, and the neutral colors (white, gray, and brown). Each color section presents five or more recipes that provide variations on a single color. For example, the yellow section includes five photographs of yellow houses, each displaying a different yellow. I isolated some of the best exterior yellow paint colors from a wide range of reputable paint manufacturers, saving you the trouble of weeding through hundreds of yellow paint chips.

Most readers will find pictured a style of house similar to their own to use as a launching point for selecting color. As you leaf through the recipes, identify photographs of homes like yours. This will help guide you with color selection, as some colors are more appropriate to certain styles than others. The exterior features on the houses in these photographs may not match yours, but if your house shares certain characteristics, such as a similar house style, you may want to consider that color recipe. For example, the exterior details of your Victorian may not match those of the Victorians in this book—yours may be simpler or more elaborate. Don't let this stop you from taking your color cues from the recipes provided.

Throughout the text, you'll find inspirational narrative and quotations that describe the mood or character each color evokes. These are meant to convey more about the style of each house and excite you about the possibility of painting.

Specific paint manufacturer color numbers are included with each recipe. Additional color options are provided for use on decorative elements (doors, shutters, window boxes, window trim, etc.). Some colors create an austere or formal look while others are playful. Although the photograph in a recipe may show a yellow house with a black door, you can, of course, decide on other door or shutter colors that suit you and the look you wish to create.

The third section of the book consists of two appendices. Appendix A (page 284) is about creating color schemes. Appendix B (page 288) is about American architecture with respect to exterior paint color.

Until now, choosing exterior paint colors meant going to the paint store, looking through paint chips or brochures, and exercising a great leap of faith. I made your task easier by sifting through the colors, carefully selecting and combining them, and showing you how they look on a house. Painting Your House Inside and Out *helps you make color choices while avoiding most of the difficulty associated with the job. This book also serves as a practical guide to the logistics of painting a house. Finally, you won't find the exterior colors in this book wildly dramatic or shockingly vivid. This is a practical guide for real people living in real homes, not a coffee-table book of unusual exteriors and show homes.*

Getting Started

Tuning In to House Color

All styles of architecture have had definable color palettes. Greek Revival and late Federal houses were predominantly white. Pale earth tones dominated early Victorian homes. Dark, rich colors ruled during the high Victorian phase and, eventually, the Colonial Revival saw a return to white and light pastels.

For our purposes, however, choosing a color scheme involves only identifying colors you like and combining them appropriately with the fixed colors surrounding your house (walkways, stone walls, roof, fences) and the nearby landscaping.

Start by looking at other houses for inspiration. Search out homes that match the architectural style of your house.

You can learn a lot from their color successes and misses. Take pictures of them. Collect photos from magazines, too, as well as exterior paint color brochures from your local paint store. Determine your color preferences. What colors attract you? Consider features of your home that may limit your paint color choices. For example, its fixed colors (brick front, stone front, terra-cotta roof, stained natural or painted wood, deck, patio, pathway, foundation) are already part of its color scheme. If these features won't be painted, they must be factored in. However, the more neutral the fixed colors are (gray shingled roof, blacktop driveway, cement foundation), the less weight they will carry in your decision. If your home is historic, your town may restrict paint color choices.

> I understand how scarlet can differ from crimson because I know that the smell of an orange is not the smell of a grapefruit. —Helen Keller

The recipes in this book offer a personal, easy, quick, and reliable approach to choosing paint colors. If you wish to do more research, look at paint color manufacturers' chips and strips. Each strip shows five to ten relative values of a color, and each manufacturer offers 1200 to 2000 colors. But not many people can visualize colors on a house using paint chips. If you go this route, compare your favorite chip colors to the colors in this book. This will help you gauge whether or not the colors are appropriate or too light, too dark, or too intense for your home. For a technical approach, see Appendix A, which describes using the color wheel to make color selections.

Fixed Features

Now that you have considered the colors of other homes, let's focus on your house, its fixed features, and its surroundings.

Let's also consider the atmosphere you wish to create. Your repainted house is a revealing public presentation of you, so it is important to spend time evaluating your house (see the following lists) before making decisions. Take the time to observe and evaluate all of the fixed features of your house. Write down any point that is applicable to you.

Stand outside and look at your house as a whole. Imagine it all white. This will help you focus on the details. How intricate are the door and window frames? Should they be emphasized? Are the windows arranged symmetrically or asymmetrically? Notice the sashes (on a double-hung window, the portions of the window that move up and down) and the number of doors and their place-

ment. Notice the roofline. Are the eaves (the projecting lower edge or edges of a roof) open or boxed? Note the patterns of brick, stone, or wood, if present on your house. Observe the location and vertical lines of the downspouts. Which lines or forms on your house, if any, would you consider emphasizing with color? Which would you rather fade into the background?

Jot down any detail that strikes you as pertinent to paint color selection. You might think the trim would look great painted in a contrasting color. Perhaps your window sashes could be painted to contrast with the trim. Evaluate their width. Are they wide enough to accent with a color? Focus your attention on the landscape colors. What colors predominate? Do you think they should affect your house paint color choices? Do you plan new landscaping?

How to Assess Fixed Features

Roof

If your roof is neutral—gray or black, for instance—you can make your color plan without regard to its color. If it is more colorful, you must include it in your overall color scheme. Identify the color of your roof. If you live in an older house, it is probably one of the following:

- slate—purple, gray-black, blue-black, purple-red, or green
- wooden shingle—brown or gray
- metal—unpainted copper, usually dark red, dark reddish-brown, or dark olive
- ceramic tile—terra-cotta, yellow, yellow to brownish-red, red, green, or blue

Newer houses usually feature composition roofing of asphalt or fiberglass in any of these colors.

Masonry

Does your home feature significant brick and stonework on the house, pathways, patios, or garden walls? Unpainted concrete is neutral, but brick and stone have plenty of color. If colored masonry is prominent, you must factor it into your color scheme. Alternatively, you can paint it as part of a new color scheme.

Downspouts and Gutters

Downspouts and gutters should almost always be inconspicuously painted. If the house trim is white, they should probably be white too. If they are copper, allow them to oxidize naturally.

Awnings

Awnings are usually made of canvas and have a color and a pattern. If their color is neutral, chances are you needn't consider them. If they are striped in blue and white, they must be factored into your color scheme.

Plants

Trees, grass, flowers, and ornamental plantings are considered fixed features. With respect to your color scheme, focus on their spring and summer colors. Bright fall foliage is fleeting, and the browns and grays of winter are neutral and, therefore, have limited effect on the color scheme.

Nature combines colors in ways that we don't dare, so choose landscape–house color combinations that please you. If a magenta rhododendron is planted close to a brown house and the colors seem out of sync, either move the plant or add more of the same to accentuate the color. There is color strength in numbers, but you must like the color combination.

Continued on next page

Continued from previous page

Other Buildings

If a shed, separated garage, barn, or doghouse is visible with your house, its materials, if they are colored, must be factored in or painted to coordinate with the main building.

Wood and Metal

Stained, varnished, or painted wood, as well as metal, should be factored into your scheme. Fences, gates, and decks, especially right next to the house, must be treated as fixed features or repainted.

Wood and metal both have color. Oak is a light- to medium-value brown; mahogany is a darker, warmer brown, and cherry is a lighter, redder brown. Though they are all basically brown, they shift toward other hues—yellow, pink, red, green, blue, etc. Iron and steel, galvanized metal, aluminum, copper, and brass also have color. If these materials are going to remain unpainted, you must treat them as fixed features when choosing paint colors.

Foundation

On most homes, the foundation is neutral in color. If yours is stone or brick and looks attractive, don't paint it. The foundation of Victorian homes was often painted a dark brick red. Their original owners didn't plant in front of them to avoid harboring insects.

Water Table

The board below the siding of clapboard buildings is called the water table. Customarily, it is painted to match the trim color.

Steps

On wooden steps, the treads (the steps themselves) usually carry the porch or deck color while the risers (the vertical pieces between the steps) are normally painted the house trim color.

Porch

Porches were traditionally painted with gray floors and blue ceilings; the reflected light was practical, and the blue suggested the sky. The gray floors also showed little dust and tracking. But porch floors can be painted any color. A good choice is the color of the housebody or trim, if not too dark or too light. Ceilings can be stained, varnished, or painted the housebody color. The trim color is a good choice for the rafters. Wooden porch posts are usually painted in the trim color. If you like, paint a decorative floor (remembering its high maintenance when it comes to repainting). Paint alternate floorboards in two colors to create stripes, or do a neoclassical checkerboard in light and dark blocks.

| **Balustrades** | Balustrades are two parallel rails, held in place by porch posts or pedestals, with the space between them occupied by a row of balusters. They enclose balconies, staircases, terraces, and so on. The balustrades are sometimes painted darker than the rails. |

| **Porch Grill or Latticework** | The grill or latticework under the porch can be painted with consideration to its size. If it is large (5–6 feet or 1.5–1.6 meters), a dark color will camouflage it. If it is short (1–3 feet or .3–.9 meters), paint it the house body color, trim color, or white. |

Windows

In the nineteenth century, window sashes and frames were usually painted the same color. Sometimes the sashes were painted darker. After 1876, sashes and frames were differentiated; the sash was painted darker, except on white Colonial Revival houses. The storm windows are always the same color as the sash.

Evaluate your windows. If they have elaborate trim (Victorian houses do), you may decide to highlight it by using a darker color on the receding or sunken parts (called shadows). If the housebody is light, painting the facings of the windows, the cornices, and so on, in a darker shade of the same color will make them seem to project outward. You could reverse this scenario by painting a lighter color on the receding or sunken parts and painting the facings of the windows in a lighter tint of the house color. If your house has detailed trim, refer to a good book on Victorian houses for accurate color selection and application.

If your windows have white vinyl trim that cannot be painted, you should probably have white house trim too.

Shutters

In the nineteenth century, shutters were essential for protection and were almost always painted dark green. Later, lighter tints or darker shades of the house color were used, with a preference for darker colors. Sometimes shutters are painted using the trim color. This is a good place to be creative.

Doors

Assess materials first: steel, wood, fiberglass, screen door, storm door. You can paint almost any material if you use the correct type of paint. Paint screen and storm doors the same color as the main door, or use the trim color. With main doors, your options are varied. You can stain and varnish them to display the natural wood grain. If your wood door isn't naturally beautiful wood, you can paint it using faux-finish graining to simulate wood. You can paint it in a contrasting color that complements the color of the house, or use the trim color. Door frames can be painted the same color as the house or the trim color. You might use a darker shade of the trim color for sunken panels on the door and a medium shade for the stiles (the vertical struts on paneled doors).

Choosing Colors

Now that you have made some important determinations about your house's fixed features and its surroundings, let us focus on methods for choosing color.

We will use the recipes in this book and their accompanying photographs. This approach is creative and enjoyable. You can also refer to Appendix A if you are interested in the color wheel approach to color scheme creation.

As you go through the recipe sections, consider how the house color, trim color, and decorative detail colors affect the mood you want your house to set in addition to whether the colors contrast or blend in with the surroundings.

Trim and detail colors always affect the character a house conveys. The colors of brick and stone can be formal and austere or familiar and gracious, depending on the paint colors used on the accompanying trim and decorative details. Imagine a brick-fronted Federal house with black shutters. Picture the same house with pale blue shutters. This change makes a difference in the overall mood the house creates. Pale blue seems friendlier than reserved black. Imagine the difference between a white clapboard house with dark green shutters and doors and the same white house with red shutters and doors. Green is the traditional shutter color choice. It is staid, blending in with its surroundings, the trees and grass. Red, being the complement of green, stands out from its surroundings. It is a more dynamic, livelier choice than green.

Four Steps for Choosing Exterior Paint Color

Step 1

General Color

Choose one or two color sections from this book to focus on based on your personal color preferences. I chose the yellow and white sections because my house is in the Colonial style and for years I have admired traditional white and yellow Colonials. I wanted a color to reflect light and look bright. Also, I felt that the colors of my landscape (lots of pink, white, blue, and red blossoms) and my fixed fixtures (a red brick walk) would stand out against a white or yellow backdrop.

Now stand outside and imagine one of the colors you selected on your house. In my case, that was white. How will it look with your fixed features, the colors of your shrubs, flowers, and so on? How will it look on your specific lot? Will it make the house stand out or blend in? How will the color look next to the homes abutting it (if they are close to your house)? Will the color work on the style of your home? Evaluate this color. Once you are satisfied that you have fully imagined it on the house, go through the same exercise using your second possible color.

Step 2

Specific Color

Narrow your choice to just one color section using step 1. In my case, I realized that a big white house would be a little too prominent on our small corner lot. The house was formerly a pale beige-brown. White was too striking a contrast. Yellow, on the other hand, was still bright and pleasant but would not overpower the house or the lot. Yellow added interest and color but was less a contrast with the landscape than white. Make these determinations for your house, and narrow your focus to just one color section.

Step 3

Reassess

Now that you know the color you will be evaluating on your house (in my case, yellow), look over all the recipes in that color section. You will see five or more houses, each painted in a variation of that color. Choose one or two of your favorite recipes from the section. Let the style of your house and the style of the houses pictured help you. Write down the paint color numbers of your favorite(s). You will test the colors you choose before painting the entire house. Often, the final colors are determined using a process of elimination at the testing stage. Pick what you think is your best choice, and take your color cues for the door and additional decorative elements from suggestions in the recipe and other houses you have observed. Don't finalize any of your trim or accompanying colors until you test your main color.

Step 4

Testing the Paint Color(s)

View the colors all together on your house. For each color you are testing, buy a quart of paint, a stir stick, and a disposable foam brush. You should also purchase a drop cloth or lay down newspaper to catch drips and spills. Sample each color directly on the house. You don't need to paint a large area—just enough to determine if you like the colors, about 2 feet by 2 feet (.6 m by .6 m). If you like a color, test it again over a larger area—about 5 feet by 5 feet (1.5 m by 1.5 m). Test the colors on doors and trim also. You don't need to paint the whole door. Paint just enough of it to determine whether the color suits you and whether the color works well with the housebody color. I cannot emphasize the importance of testing colors directly on the house enough. This is the only way to assess how they will actually look. Testing colors on a board or posterboard is inadequate. Believe me, I am speaking from experience.

Colors look different on a house than on chips. In addition, the same color paint will look different on clapboard than it does on wooden shingles. It will look different in the sun than it does in the shade (because light affects color), so apply tests in sunny and shady areas. View these test patches at different times of the day. Apply at least two coats of paint for your test patches. Wait for paint to dry completely before making a decision. Latex reaches its true color in one hour, alkyd (oil) in 24 hours.

If you are basically satisfied with a color but want to make subtle adjustments, don't hesitate to ask for help. Paint dealers can lighten, darken, or temper your colors. This testing and adjusting is worth your time and effort. Don't let impatience get the better of you. Make sure you are satisfied before investing in paint, labor, and money.

Once your paint dealer makes the color adjustments (if any), test your colors on the house again until they meet your satisfaction. Now you are ready to paint the house. If you find that the color simply doesn't work the way you had hoped, move on. Choose another color to evaluate and repeat these steps.

Keep in mind that the photographs on these pages have undergone a printing process that alters their actual color. Therefore, while you can use these photos as a guide to determine your color preferences, rely on the actual paint chip color numbers, the corresponding chips found at your paint dealership, and your color test to make your final decisions.

Painting the House

Hiring a Painter

If you are hiring a painter, get two or three estimates. Ask friends and neighbors, as well as your local paint store, for referrals.

You want someone who can do a great job at a price you can afford and with whom you are comfortable working. Ask the paint contractors the following questions before they visit your house:

1. Are you licensed? Make sure the painter you hire is licensed. This gives you some protection if you are not happy with the work. Each state has its own standards of performance for paint contractors and has different means of addressing customer grievances.

2. Do you have insurance? Your painter should carry liability insurance. In the event that your property is damaged, you will have the security that the contractor is responsible for fixing it.

3. Do you guarantee your work? Your painter should guarantee his work. Paint manufacturers guarantee their paint up to twenty years. Weather, quality of materials, and excellent prep determine how long the paint will last.

4. Who will do the work? Some companies bid out paint jobs to other contractors. You want to know who is actually doing the work and be sure that the supervisor on the job understands the job. You also must ensure that the subcontract is exactly the same as the original contract to which you agreed. You need to be comfortable working with the supervisor.

5. What is your preferred brand of paint? Many painters use one brand of paint exclusively. If you have a different preference, ask the painter if he is willing use it. Often, painters will offer to match paint colors in your preferred brand using their brand. A perfect match is impossible, and even subtle color changes make a huge difference on an area as large as a house, so beware.

Once you receive the estimates and decide on a painter, arrange a written schedule for the work and the payment. Don't assume that your painters will start and finish your job before moving on to the next. Many painters juggle multiple jobs at once. They may show up at your house on day one and not again for two weeks. Painting does depend on the weather, so make allowances for rain.

Be sure to agree to, and list in writing, any special requests that you have, such as daily starting and quitting times, whether you permit use of a radio, disposing of paint, cleanup requirements, even whether dogs or kids are allowed on the job (you'd be surprised).

Calculating the Size of Your House

The best way to assess a contractor's estimate is to approximate one yourself. Whether you do your own work or not, you should estimate the amount of time and materials needed. Use these simple guidelines:

Step 1

Calculate the size of the house.

1. Measure the width of the house.	Run a tape measure along the base.
2. Measure the height of the house.	To measure the height of a two-story house, pick a point about half way up, measure to that point, then double the result.
3. Calculate the square footage of the house.	You don't need to make deductions for doors, as there are only a few. Use common sense to deduct footage for windows. Make adjustments for large surfaces on the house not to be painted.

Step 2

Estimate time.

Aside from the actual painting, you need to include time for daily setup, cleanup, breaks, meals, runs to store for materials, and weather interruptions.

Housebody	for a painter to roll and brush smooth siding (e.g., clapboard) on a house:	100–150 square feet (30.5–45.7 m)/hour
	for a painter to roll and brush a medium-textured stucco wall:	200 square feet (61 m)/hour
	for a painter to roll and brush shingles:	80–125 square feet (24.4–38.1 m)/hour
Windows *calculated by the number of panes, or lights, of glass*	ordinary sash window: (1 light over 1 light):	20 minutes
	ordinary sash window: (6 lights over 1 light):	40 minutes
	ordinary sash window: (12 lights):	60 minutes
Doors *standard sizes*	plain:	15 minutes
	paneled:	45 minutes
	louvered:	45 minutes
Miscellaneous	louvered shutters, 2 feet by 4 feet (.6 m by 1.2 m) (both sides):	45 minutes
	simple wrought-iron railing:	20 linear feet (6.1 m)/hour
	decorated wrought-iron railing:	10 linear feet (3 m)/hour
	simple wooden railing:	15 linear feet (4.6 m)/hour
	wide eaves:	50 square feet (15.2 m)/hour

Step 3

Estimate materials.

Paint coverage depends on the porosity of the surface it is deposited on. Obviously, unpainted plaster is more porous than primed wood. The following figures are for a surface of average porosity.

Acrylic (latex) paint (square yards/square meter)		**Oil-based (alkyd) paint** (square yards/square meter)	
primer/undercoat:	55 (46 sq. m)	primer:	110 (92 sq. m)
paint finish coat:	82 (69 sq. m)	undercoat:	82 (69 sq. m)
masonry paint (smooth surface):	65 (54 sq. m)	paint finish coat:	92 (76 sq. m)
masonry paint (rough surface):	22 (18 sq. m)	oil:	65 (54 sq. m)
wood stain:	110 (92 sq. m)	wood preservative:	55 (46 sq. m)
		varnish:	87 (73 sq. m)
		wood stain:	120 (100 sq. m)

Choosing
Paint and Stain

Whether you choose to paint or stain, buy high-quality materials. Low-cost paint that yields poor coverage can end in disaster.

It's better to start with good materials. You will need to determine the sheen best suited for each of the surfaces to be painted (high gloss, semigloss, flat, etc.). Every paint brand has its own terms for these sheens. Gloss or sheen is the degree to which a painted surface reflects light. High gloss, semigloss, satin finish, eggshell, low luster, and matte (or flat) finish are typical names for a manufacturer's glosses.

- High gloss looks wet and shiny.
- Semigloss is shiny and smooth but not wet looking. It is the most common sheen used for trim.
- Eggshell, satin, and low luster fall in the middle between flat and high gloss.
- Matte or flat finish looks like unglazed tile or chalk.

Choosing the level of gloss is an aesthetic decision. Be aware, however, that high gloss shows imperfections more than any other sheen and, therefore, requires more careful preparation. Time and weather reduce the gloss level.

You must further choose among the following three types of paint:

1. oil-based paint, in which the vehicle or binder is a drying oil, such as linlinseed or soy
2. latex paint, in which the vehicle is a water-based emulsion
3. solvent products, including varnishes and specialty finishes

All paint products go from a liquid state through various stages of drying to a full cure. Many oil-based paints must be dry for six, eight, or up to twenty-four hours before recoating. Latex requires between one and three hours.

Paint and Stain Options

Latex	The main advantages of latex are low odor, easy cleanup, short drying time, superior build, and low sensitivity to alkali in the surface, which is important when painting over cement or plaster.
Oil	Although oil-based paints take longer to dry, they dry harder than latex, hold much better, are impermeable, and are more resistant to abrasion.
Alkyd-modified latex	These latex house paints contain modified alkyd resins and offer the best of both worlds—latex and oil.
Stain	Stains contain the same basic ingredients as paint and are applied in the same way. They are also available in latex and oil-based versions. Whereas paint is solid and opaque, stain penetrates the surface to reveal the natural color and texture of wood. Natural stains make the least change in the color of the wood because they have the least pigment. When using stain, there is no need to smooth or prime the surface wood. Stain doesn't last as long as paint because it has less build.
Semitransparent stain	These stains have more pigment than natural stains but still allow some natural color to show through.
Opaque stain	These stains have enough pigment to make solid colors but allow more natural texture of the surface to show than paint does. They also produce the lowest sheen available.
Penetrating color sealer	Clear or tinted, these stains correspond to transparent interior wood stains for use on new or unfinished wood or wood previously treated with the same product.
Porch and deck paint	Surfaces subject to extra-heavy wear (including thresholds) should be painted with a product specifically formulated to resist abrasion and foot traffic. These paints are available in latex and oil-based formulations.

(Note: Redwood and cedar contain water-soluble substances that can stain through latex paints. They must be sealed with an oil-based product before they can be painted with latex.)

Preparation before Painting

Proper surface preparation is the most critical part of the paint job.

If your house is in good shape and you are only changing the color, preparation should take only one-half or one-quarter of the time it takes to apply one coat of paint to the house. If, however, there is peeling paint or deterioration, the prep time will be longer—about the same time as it takes to apply one coat of paint. If paint is peeling over a small part of the house, remove the loose paint, spot prime, and apply the finish coat. This approach may take as long as applying one full coat of paint to the house. If you want to make the house look like new, scrape and prime the entire house. Applying this coat of primer would not count as prep time because you are actually painting the entire house with it. It would be calculated as paint time.

If you have good prep work, the new paint will adhere to the building for five years or more. If you have poor prep, the paint job will last only about two years. Basic prep includes these tasks:

- Protect plants, window glass, and other unpainted surfaces.
- Power wash the house.
- Kill mildew.
- Remove loose paint, spot prime bare wood, and spot prime metal on the same day (to prevent rusting).
- Smooth surface by sanding or stripping old paint.
- Repair loose or missing glazing from windows before priming.
- Etch, clean, and prime bare galvanized steel with metal primer.
- Patch holes and cracks in wood, stucco, and metal, then sand patches smooth.
- Caulk.
- Apply full coat of primer if necessary.

Primers

The primer provides a surface for paint to adhere to. It also protects and seals the surface. You can tint the primer using your base color for better paint color coverage. Tint the primer slightly lighter than the base coat color (so as not to confuse them). Once you have primed the house, you must paint soon after (within weeks is best), as primer should not be exposed to weather for long. Some primers can be applied and finish coated the same day. Many need twenty-four hours to cure. Discuss the type of primer to use with your paint dealer.

(Note: Each metal surface has its own preparation requirements. Talk with your paint dealer.)

Masonry Prep

Most masonry finishes have a life expectancy of up to ten years. However, without good surface preparation, that may be cut in half. Masonry prep involves these tasks:

- Scrape loose materials, such as paint and lichen.
- Check for mold and algae and apply fungicide (allow twenty-four hours for fungicide to kill mold), then wash with clean water.
- When walls are dry, rub your hand across them to check for chalky or powdery texture. Treat those areas with a stabilizing solution to bind the surface and make it ready to accept paint.
- Repair any surface flaw larger than a hairline crack with exterior filler or cement, depending on the severity of the cracks or holes.
- Prime with masonry primer.

Common Problems Requiring Prep

Chalking	Existing paint looks like it has a layer of chalk dust. Run your finger across it. If you pick up a layer of residue, you will need to wash the house with trisodium phosphate (TSP) or another strong detergent. Work from the top down with a scrub brush or use a power washer.
Mildew	Wash mildewed areas with chlorine bleach solution and soap. Use 3 parts soapy water to I part bleach.
Metal stains	Wash stains off wood before priming. Prime metal before painting to keep stain from bleeding onto wood.
Rot	Dry or wet rot must be removed or killed with a biocide. Patch holes. Stabilize damage with resinous wood hardener. Patch with resin fillers.
Knots	Spot prime knots with pigmented shellac (latex or oil-based) to seal out the resin.
Nail holes	Fill with exterior spackle compound or linseed oil putty.
Uneven, chipped, or peeling paint	Scrape (go with the grain) and sand or strip if necessary before priming using a heat gun or chemical stripper.
Cracks	Use exterior spackle compound to fill small cracks in wood siding, cracks or gaps between different kinds of building materials (e.g., wood and masonry, wood and metal, plastic and metal; also joints between two pieces of wood in a window or door frame), and small cracks in stucco. Repair large cracks in stucco with stucco patch. Repair large cracks in wood with resin fillers.
Cracked window glazing	If window glaze has shallow surface cracks, add new glazing compound over it. If glaze is badly cracked, use a heat gun to remove old compound back to a clean sash, prime, and reglaze the window.
Alligatoring and crazing	These paint conditions are caused by paint drying faster than it should or by putting on too thick a coat of paint. Scrape, sand, and patch affected areas before priming.

Blistering	This condition is caused by painting over surface dirt or moist wood. Moisture is trying to escape from behind the paint. Scrape and sand affected areas before priming.
Efflorescence	This condition, in which salts crystallize on a masonry surface, is caused by mineral salts reacting with water. Scrape away deposits and let dry completely. Use only water-based paints, which allow remaining water or moisture to dry through the painted surface.
Loose plaster	The plaster layer on a wall sometimes breaks away from its blockbase, making the wall surface unstable. Plaster tends to break down in localized areas. Loose plaster should always be removed and the surface patched.
Rust stains	This brownish staining is caused by external metal fixtures or old nails that corrode and wash down masonry walls in the rain. Paint all metal fixtures, then clean stained areas and seal them with an oil-based undercoat.

Preparation Tips for Metal and Vinyl

Vinyl gutters	No primer needed. Use one or two coats of gloss paint.
Metal gutters	Use commercial metal paints for all except aluminum.
Metal windows	Use metal primer.
Aluminum and vinyl windows	Do not paint.
Galvanized metals	Use specially designed primer.
Metal garage doors	Use metal primer, undercoat, then one or two coats of gloss paint.

Painting

To be sure that your primer and paint will bond to the surface paint, paint in the right weather—mild and dry. Don't paint in direct sunlight. Start early in the day so paint can dry before the evening dew falls. The ideal conditions are 70°F (21°C) with little to no breeze.

Paint the house in this order:

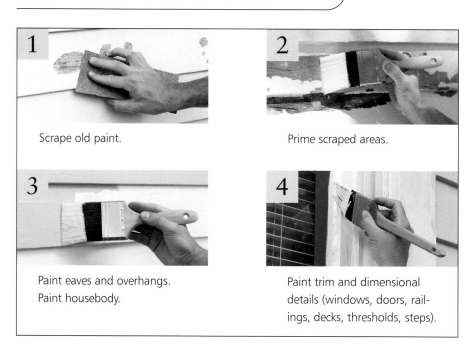

1 Scrape old paint.

2 Prime scraped areas.

3 Paint eaves and overhangs. Paint housebody.

4 Paint trim and dimensional details (windows, doors, railings, decks, thresholds, steps).

For all surfaces:

- Work from the top down and the inside out.
- Apply flat paints before gloss paints, as they are easier to touch up than gloss.
- Save areas to be stained for last.
- Reach a visual breakpoint before you stop painting, especially for gloss finishes.
- Paint doors and windows early in the day so they will dry before being closed and locked at night.
- Let one color dry before painting another next to it.

Apply all exterior finishes in the right order

Alkyd Paint on Bare Wood	1. bare wood 2. sealer on bare wood knots 3. primer or preservative primer 4. undercoat 5. paint
Latex Paint on Bare Wood	1. bare wood 2. sealer on bare wood knots 3. primer undercoat 4. paint
Masonry Paint on New Plaster	1. bare plaster 2. first coat masonry paint 3. second coat masonry paint
Masonry Paint on Old Plaster	1. old painted masonry surface 2. fungicide 3. stabilizing solution/primer 4. first coat masonry paint 5. second coat masonry paint
Wood Stain	1. bare wood 2. preservative base coat (solvent-based products only) 3. first coat stain 4. second coat stain (third coat may be required for water-based products)
Varnish	1. bare wood 2. preservative base coat 3. first coat varnish 4. second coat varnish
Metal Finishing Paint	1. bare or previously painted metal 2. first coat proprietary metal finishing paint 3. second coat metal finishing paint if necessary

Finally, be sure to keep some of the paint and finish that you use for touch-ups or to match colors later.

Red is the great clarifier—

bright, cleansing, and revealing. It makes all colors look beautiful.

I can't imagine getting bored with red—it would be like getting

bored with the person you love. —Diana Vreeland

Red houses look beautiful all year in their surroundings. During the winter, red houses are warm and lively against the white snow, beckoning us to enter. In summer, red houses are highlighted by fresh green lawns, draping foliage, and blossoming bushes. Red houses glow in the sunlight among the colors of fall foliage—crimson, gold, and amber.

From brick to ruby, there is a red for every architectural style. Whether you live in a Vermont-style farmhouse, a Gothic, Spanish, art deco, Victorian, or Dutch Colonial, red is a fabulous paint color choice. Reds range from hot crimson and scarlet to cherry, cranberry, and clay, and on into pink. It takes confidence to paint your house red, but lovers of red tend to be self-assured and secure individuals to begin with.

Care to lighten up? Pink is friendly, even playful, and tells your visitors that hospitality lies within. Some pinks are whimsical—tropic pinks and cotton candy. Other desirable pinks are elegant rose and friendly magenta. If your house is stucco, try a light rose with gray-green trim to evoke the Caribbean, the Greek isles, or Florida's South Beach. A dramatic statement can be made by painting a wood clapboard house raspberry with black shutters and white trim.

If you are not up to painting your whole house red, create a focal point by painting it on the front door. Berry red is a lovely welcome to guests and is recommended by practitioners of the ancient Chinese art of feng shui as a front door color because it invites prosperity. You can choose to paint the shutters red to create a cottage look. How about red deck paint on your porch? There are many places red can work its magic.

Use your imagination as you go through the recipes that follow. You'll love being "the neighbor in the red house!"

Raspberry Jewel Deep Violet Red

Simple things become beautiful and attractive by an art inspiration. Homes retain their old forms substantially, but they put on new faces when touched by the real artist.

—Palliser, *Palliser's American Architecture*, 1888

Sometimes the gray days of winter feel so long. Spring seems elusive. And then you see something beautiful that renews your spirit—COLOR! The color of raspberries. It is the dead of winter, yet this heartwarming red-raspberry house stands in vibrant contrast to the white snow, reminding us of the importance of well-chosen color.

The raspberry clapboard is perfectly complemented by the blue-green door and window sashes. The house attains a complete visual balance through its inherent symmetry and its carefully chosen color scheme. The cream-colored window frames, eaves, and door panels provide contrast and make the raspberry and blue-green house colors pop. Stenciled patterns on the door panels and a thick boxwood garland draped around the door add elegance to the otherwise simple facade of this Colonial house.

Fixed features include the granite steps, walk, and stone wall—all gray, with hints of blue. The blue door color picks up the tones of these elements. Landscaping in the front yard is primarily green shrubbery echoing the blue-green of the door, with white accents. In spring and summer, assorted flowers are displayed in decorative pots. This is a truly wonderful combination. No additional colors are necessary.

1

2

3

Perfectly Painted:

To add charm to your home, add decorative painting to the front door, such as this stenciled door panel.

Housebody color:	1. Benjamin Moore—Old Claret 2083-30	
Trim color:	2. Benjamin Moore—Monterey White HC-27	
Details:	3. Benjamin Moore—Crystal Lake 353-4	

For a Different Look

If this house color is too bright, daring, or edgy for your tastes, choose a less purple red. A redder red will still look beautiful, but will have a slightly more traditional appearance. Door and trim colors can remain the same.

Enigmatic Pink

Rose Blush

The very pink of perfection. —Oliver Goldsmith

This old Victorian extravaganza looks perky in pink. It expresses both lightheartedness and a sense of solidity and sturdiness. Pink gives a whimsical lift but still exemplifies a rather sophisticated color choice. Why does the house seem to elicit such contradictory reactions? Because pink has a split personality. Pink consists of red and white, and each of these colors causes different reactions. Bluer pinks take on many of the serene qualities of blue. Likewise, redder pinks take on the dynamic qualities of red. Add gray to the mix, and the color becomes subdued and low-key. Pink conjures a wide variety of reactions in everyone who views it. How does it strike you? Isn't it a great way to enliven the house?

An engaging personality is inherent in this extraordinary color. Try this approach to making your home both unusual and attractive. Landscape with lots of evergreens and coordinating colors such as violet and blue.

Housebody color:	1. Benjamin Moore—Pink Petals 2085-60
Trim color:	2. Benjamin Moore—Brilliant White
Details:	3. Benjamin Moore—Gypsy Love 2085-30 on door and details
	4. Benjamin Moore—Old Pickup Blue 2054-60

For a Different Look

Use colors from the existing recipe, and decide which colors to emphasize by featuring them on the architectural elements of your choice. For instance, you might choose a white door and colored trim rather than the white trim and a colored door.

Perfectly Painted:

Choose two or three colors to accentuate the details on a particularly interesting element, such as a carving. You could, for instance, use a darker shade of a single color on the underside or flat part of the surface to emphasize the depth of the carving.

Farmhouse
Red Darkest Berry

I saw the spiders marching through the air,

   swimming from tree to tree that mildewed day

In latter August when the hay

Came creaking to the barn... .

—Robert Lowell, "Mr. Edwards and the Spider"

The settling of America was a utopian adventure for many Europeans. It was a new beginning, yet they brought their color sense with them. This was reflected in the paint colors used on their homes. Colonial settlers were dependent on imported blocks of dried pigment for these colors. They were expensive, so most homeowners, especially those in rural areas, relied on local colors ground from the earth, plants, and berries. This explains why red houses seem to organically blend with their environments.

This red house is painted in keeping with these historic origins. The simple split rail fence adds interest to this rustic home.

Consider your house. Is it clapboard or shingle? Such traditional red looks best on clapboard. What size is your home? If too large a surface area is painted red, the effect will become overwhelming. Complement the main portion of the house with neutral elements on smaller sections of the house, such as shake shingling or stone on the garage or breezeway. In this case, where the main portion of the house is of moderate size, there is no denying red looks great.

Housebody and trim color:	1. California Paints—Roasted Pepper AC116N
Details:	2. California Paints—Old Porch 8636N

For a Different Look
The door color in this recipe is subdued. You can bring more color into this scheme simply by painting the door green rather than this charcoal color. A green door is a less restrained, more colorful alternative.

Perfectly Painted:

Generally speaking, the less complex the trimming on a house, the fewer colors you will use.

Pink Surprise Dusty Pink

The essential elements…of the romantic spirit are curiosity and the love of beauty.

—Walter Pater

This house is an appealing combination of dusty pink, gray, and cream. The colors bring an element of surprise and sparkle to the neighborhood. Notice that the stairs, window frames, and some decorative detailing echo the gray of the roof shingle. This is appropriate, given that the shingle is itself decorative. Cream trim frames and highlights the pink and gray. Green foliage complements and softens the hard lines of the house.

This dusty pink is gentle and muted. It is sophisticated, upscale, and even romantic. The gray detailing keeps it looking grounded. Even if your home does not feature such intricate detailing, this combination of colors could play up those interesting elements that are present.

If you are a plant lover, get out your garden tools. The color pink has been shown to influence the growth of plants. Plants grown in pink hothouses actually grow twice as fast and are sturdier than those grown in blue hothouses.

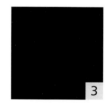

Housebody color:	1. Sherwin-Williams—Pink Prelude SW2295
Trim color:	2. Sherwin-Williams—Classical White SW2829
Details:	3. Sherwin-Williams—Tricorn Black SW2126 on details and door trim
	4. Sherwin-Williams—Stonecutter SW2124 on door and trim details
	5. Sherwin-Williams—Roseroot SW2711 on trim details

For a Different Look
Try using the trim color from this recipe, Rosewood, on the door. It will give the house more sparkle without changing the color scheme at all.

Perfectly Painted:

Paint carved wooden details with one main color and up to three accent colors.

Rustic Red Barn Red

The wilderness provides that perfect relaxation which all jaded minds require.

—William H. H. Murrays

Normally, we think of red as a color that packs a punch—that jumps out at us and excites. This red house is anything but that. Instead, it exemplifies the height of serenity and calm. This is partly due to the choice of red—a deep brick color—and also a result of pairing the color with natural wood and other natural, neutral elements.

This red is great on houses with shingles or wood clapboard. To ensure that it feels restful and interesting, be sure to use a combination of materials. Include natural wood in the color scheme. For example, you might include a wooden porch, deck, or staircase, and gravel or pea-stone paths and driveway.

This house is extraordinarily special because it incorporates actual trees in the architecture—as columns on the porch. Red painted trim on the porch door also enlivens the look. Window trim can be painted red or green, as seen here.

Your house doesn't need to have these embellishments to be attractive in red. This paint color will work on the most ordinary house. Keep the landscaping simple—greens with a few hints of color.

The wonder of this house is how ingeniously a rather ordinary structure is at once made to feel contemporary and rustic.

Housebody and trim color:	1. Benjamin Moore—Heritage Red
Details:	Natural wood and green trim on windows

For a Different Look

For an even more rustic, woodsy look, you can eliminate the green window trim, and instead use the Heritage Red house body color on the window trim. For a hint of contrast and some added interest, use green paint on the door frame. The house will maintain its warm, serene quality.

Music Man

Creamy Pink

A songwriter is really a journalist of the time with music. —Edgar Yipsel Harburg

Here is the quintessential example of Americana—a neat and tidy, creamy Victorian house with white trim. It conjures up images of *The Music Man*—you can almost imagine folks strolling down perfectly manicured streets, eating ice cream cones on a sunny summer day.

The color of the house is highlighted with the addition of pale pink gingerbread cutout shingles, dashes of red on the flag, and hanging potted geraniums. The neutral gray steps and porch maintain a soft look.

As for details, you can keep it simple, like this homeowner did, by sporting a natural wood door—or, for a more dazzling effect, you can paint the door—not the screen door) a vibrant red or orange, or a lovely blue, framed with white moldings. This will give the house a much more playful and dynamic look.

The landscaping is monochrome green. A neutral background is capable of sustaining all the colors of the rainbow. So you can get as creative as you wish with your choice of affinity and landscape colors.

Housebody color:	1. Benjamin Moore—Odessa Pink HC-60 on gingerbread-style shingles; natural stain on door
Trim color:	2. Benjamin Moore—White

For a Different Look
Nothing is friendlier than a bright blue-, wild cherry-, or tangerine-colored door. All of these color choices make this house a more welcoming house. Depending on the shade that you choose, a colored door can add an otherwise absent air of whimsy.

1

2

Perfectly Painted:

If you have a textured house, the color you paint over it can make

the texture seem more or less apparent; choose carefully.

Red Detailing

Do you love red but worry about painting the whole house? You can get enormous impact from red even if you only use it on the doors, the trim, or on decorative elements, such as benches that have been placed beside the house. Here are a few striking samples.

Left:
Feel the excitement that red elicits on this otherwise neutral shingled home. If you prefer an earthy color for your house but wish to create a dynamic, exciting facade, consider painting the trim red. This bold crimson commands your attention without upsetting the down to earth quality of this home.

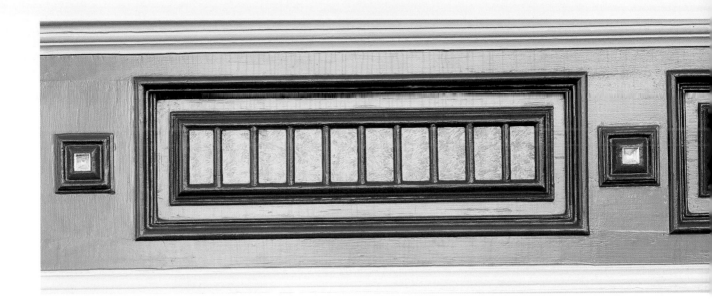

Above:
Red accents on this cobalt blue panel add interest and life, while drawing attention to the faux-marble finish and touches of gold. Consider this treatment to make a house sparkle.

Left:
The entrance to this West Coast Victorian comes to life with some well-placed splashes of deep cranberry. The red, white, and dark blue details become the focal point on a soothing gray background.

The triumphant colorist

has only to appear. We have prepared his

palette for him. —Paul Signac

Orange is the sunset, finely finished wood, sherbet, the center of a squash, a roaring fire, and a hillside in autumn. We are mesmerized by the sight of it. We all love peach, coral, salmon, gold, and amber.

When you imagine an orange house, a home in Santa Fe may come to mind. Perhaps your imagination travels to the warm climates of the Mediterranean or Mexico. But you needn't feel limited by your location. Orange also works in any locale, bringing sunny, tranquil luminosity to a home.

Chances are, if you choose to paint your house orange, you are good-natured with a bright disposition, adventurous, and enthusiastic. Don't worry about blending in; orange ties in well with the landscape colors of all four seasons.

Orange can feel startling if not chosen properly. These recipes are good guidelines for choosing subtle shades. The safest oranges are in either the deeper shades of orange-brown or the gentler, paler tints, such as peach, apricot, and cantaloupe.

Venture into this new territory when thinking about color. Adorned with orange, your home will be a splendid, radiating jewel in the afternoon light.

Radiant Orange Bright, Dynamic

The dreams which accompany all human actions should be nurtured

by the places in which people live. —Charles W. Moore

Who says you can't paint your house orange? Just look at this stunning example. What a wonderful case of a standard box-style Colonial turned into a show house simply with paint. And to think, Americans have used this color on exteriors since this Essex, Massachusetts house was built in 1730. Orange attracts us like a magnet. Turn your somber house into a stunning attention-getter.

If you prefer a more dressed-up home, add paneled shutters painted a deep gloss green or red. Paint the front door the same color and add a natural wood stained storm door over it. Plain or dressy, this friendly orange house will brighten anyone's day.

1   2   3

Housebody color:	1. Pittsburgh Paints—Buffalo Trail 219-5
Trim color:	2. Pittsburgh Paints—Super White 88-45
Details:	3. Pittsburgh Paints—Walnut Grove 511-7 on door

For a Different Look

A high-gloss forest green or chrome red door will dress up this house without changing its simplicity. For added elegance, take this one step further—add shutters, and paint them the same color as the door.

Perfectly Painted:

Add a band of contrasting color along the roofline to bring out the shape of the house.

Song of the Broad Axe

Soft, Creamy Pale Apricot

The house-builder at work...the preparatory jointing, squaring, sawing, mortising, the hoist-up of beams, the push of them in their places, laying them regular, setting the studs by their tenons in the mortises according as they were prepared, the blows of mallets and hammers, the attitudes of the men, their curv'd limbs, bending, standing astride the pins, holding on by posts and braces, the hook'd arm over the plate, the other arm wielding the axe...their postures bringing their weapons downward on the bearers, the echoes resounding. —Walt Whitman, "Song of a Carpenter"

Few architectural styles offer the elegant simplicity of the eighteenth-century New England home, which is modest in design, uncomplicated, and stark. This circa 1750 pale apricot house with yellow trimmings glows with warmth, even on the drabbest winter days. It stands in contrast to the leafless tree limbs of winter that encompass it and offers warmth against the frequent white snows. Orange and yellow blend naturally with autumn's colors and complement the lush green foliage of spring and summer—great color choices for any time of year.

This particular orange paint color flies in the face of tradition. White-washing was the earliest form of house painting in America. However, by the mid-eighteenth century, American paint makers were mixing a wide range of colors. Yellow and umber were among the most commonly used.

This house has few fixed features. Those that exist are neutral and need not be considered in the overall color scheme. Plantings are sparse and also neutral. The pale apricot paint color is what makes this home striking. It is just unusual enough to grab your attention, yet subtle, so the simplicity of the property is retained.

The ever-changing daylight plays on this pale color and ensures a handsome start and finish to every day.

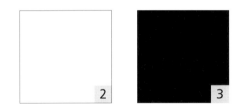

Housebody color: 1. Benjamin Moore—Asbury Sand 2156-50

Trim colors: 2. Benjamin Moore—Montgomery White

Details: 3. Benjamin Moore—Black on doors

For a Different Look

For more visual interest, try a colored door rather than black.
Deep green or red tones work nicely with the apricot house body
color. Either color would add sparkle to this house.

California Contemporary

Dusty Orange

Architecture must have integrity, like a friend. —I. M. Pei

This stunning contemporary stucco residence is marvelous in orange. Gray columns and multiple neutral architectural elements lead the eye from the house to the threshold of nature. Colors and textures combine to make a successful whole.

This strongly linear building, which might have appeared stark in gray or white, is instead made a lively work of art by brilliant orange and violet-gray. Orange is intensified by sunlight and is dramatic against a bright blue sky. The choice of violet-gray or blue-gray is drawn from the undertones of stone and cement. Thin black trim is used to accentuate windows. Should you prefer to play down contrast, you could use white instead. This combination, however, makes the most of complementary colors, architectural features, and harmony with nature.

1

2

3

Housebody color:	1. California Paints—Glazed Carrot 7326A
Trim color:	2. California Paints—Pretty Purple 7973M
Details:	California Paints—Pretty Purple 7973M on doors; 3. Black on window frames

For a Different Look

For a more colorful, daring look, consider a deep indigo blue or violet as your trim and door color. The existing gray doors and trim on this house merely hint at violet. Using deep, dark shades of violet will have a greater impact without changing the overall subtlety of the look of the house.

Perfectly Painted:

Accent a window by combining two colors—one on the sash and one on the trim.

Orange Detailing

Do you love orange but worry about painting the whole house? Orange makes a bold and welcoming statement even if used only sparingly. Perhaps consider orange just for the front door. Here are a few examples of orange detailing.

Above:

Orange is less intense than red and has more of the sunny qualities of yellow. Hot and luminous, orange is a gregarious, extrovert-
ed front door color. Coupled with this cool, turquoise porch, it
makes for a nicely balanced but dramatic and soulful entrance.
This combination of colors is reminiscent of the autumn harvest—
blue October skies, brown and burnt orange. What a friendly welcome to a deep, dark brown house. This is an adventurous color
statement for the assertive homeowner.

Left:

Orange trim keeps this Victorian from blending in with the crowd,
and its vibrant color scheme really pops. While it may be overwhelming for some people, attention-getting orange can be a
great choice for the vivacious extroverts among us.

Oh, what a beautiful mornin'

Oh, what a beautiful day.

I got a beautiful feelin'

Everything's going my way.

—Oscar Hammerstein II, from *Oklahoma!*

Yellow is seen by many as the happiest of all colors. If you are thinking of painting your house yellow, you are probably warm and optimistic, with a sunny disposition. Yellow creates an instantly cheerful and sunny family greeting. It is the perfect color for lifting spirits and, therefore, an excellent choice for climates with many gray days.

Consider the use of these yellows if your house is shingle, wood, or aluminum siding—buttery or creamy yellow, canary yellow, mellow amber yellow, even mustard yellow. Yellow is also seen on stucco houses in Florida and California, where the styles are often Spanish hacienda, Mediterranean, and Italian villa.

Yellow is an especially friendly front door color. Just imagine a dazzling lemon-yellow door and gleaming white trim on a rainy day. A yellow door is a great treatment for cedar shake or natural shingle houses. Picture sparkling chrome-yellow shutters on a white clapboard house. What a great accent! How about a golden yellow house with red trim? Or emerald-green trim on a bright yellow farmhouse to tie the building into its surrounding landscape?

Yellow is one of the most versatile colors for homes of any style and in any climate. And there are so many possibilities to choose from. To avoid a yellow oops, follow the guidelines in the recipes that follow. For the skittish, yellow is the safest color choice outside the neutrals.

Housebody color:	1. Benjamin Moore—Cream Yellow 2155-60
Trim color:	2. Benjamin Moore—Dove White
Details:	3. Benjamin Moore—Black on door and shutters

For a Different Look

You can create more color interest by adding red shutters. This is a bold statement and will change the character of the house, so be sure to test your red on one or two sets of shutters before painting them all. Another attractive treatment, and one that will not change the character of the house, is to paint the door and shutters a pleasant shade of green—you decide how light or dark.

Village Home

Butter Cream

The days are short, the weather's cold, by tavern fires tales are told.

—New England Almanac, Dec. 1704

Imagine strolling into town on a still winter day, passing pretty home after pretty home, many dating to the 1700s and 1800s. Icicles hang over the eaves. Shrubs and rooftops are dusted with snow. Leafless maple and oak trees filter the light. You are approaching a quaint and charming village where you plan to stop for a cup of hot tea and reflect on your day.

This yellow village home has the charm of a bygone era and the clean lines of a brand new house. It was built at the turn of the century—the twenty-first century, that is. It sits on a small lot with limited frontage on a busy road close to the village center. It is stunning in its architectural simplicity, and the paint colors chosen for it couldn't be more suitable. Decorative embellishments, such as brass fixtures on the front door and the festive holiday fruit decoration over it, add elegance to this sweet home.

This yellow is moderately vivid. It seems brighter in contrast with the high-gloss black shutters and door. The fixed features are the neutral granite steps and walk. This recipe works equally well with brick walk and steps. Green foliage with pink, magenta, and white blossoms is particularly beautiful against the background of this yellow house.

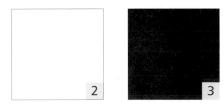

Winter Solstice Bright Chrome Yellow

Snow...makes one think not of a clean slate, a glorious future, but of a happy past and never mind that the past never really was like that. —Paul Goldberger

The Colonial house has been a fixture of residential architecture in America since the arrival of the first European settlers. A two-story clapboard box with a center chimney, this classic yellow Colonial is like countless homes of today seen in virtually every area of the country. It is a representative sample.

What makes this home distinctive is its brilliant yellow color, which resonates against a bright blue sky or bright white snow. Gloss black shutters heighten the effect. A chrome-yellow house is an especially welcome site on a dark night when lit from the outside. Yellow is compatible with virtually all colors that typically surround a house, making it a suitable paint color choice for your Colonial during any season. This home has classic, simple shrubs and evergreens. During spring and summer, potted flowers add color to the front facade. Brick walks and the neutral driveway are subtle and relatively unnoticeable.

Make your Colonial home special. Set it apart from all others with your paint color choice. Consider this wonderful yellow and enjoy its cheerfulness all year round. You may choose to paint shutters black or green and highlight the front door with still another color. Use your creativity.

1   2   3

Housebody color:	1. California Paints Historic Colors of America—Pale Organza
Trim color:	2. California Paints—White
Details:	3. California Paints—Black

For a Different Look

Dark green shutters make a traditional yellow house even more traditional. Perhaps you prefer this look over black shutters on this house. For a more dynamic, less traditional look, try a nice red on the shutters. Regardless of the shutter color, you can leave the door color black if desired.

Perfectly Painted:

Classic architectural styles lend themselves to classic combinations, such as this yellow house paint combined with gloss black on shutters.

Golden Yellow

Rich, Mellow Gold

On entering some of our villages, the only color which meets the eye is white.

Everything is white; the houses, the fences, the stables, the kennels, and sometimes

even the trees cannot escape, but get a coat of white wash...Is this taste? Whether

it be or not, one thing is certain, that a great change is coming over our people in

this respect. They are beginning to see that there are beauties in color as well as form.

—Samuel Sloan, 1852

This cozy shingled home is adorable painted all in gold. The color has a rich, burnished quality. The house projects a modest dignity. A dark red painted chimney and freshly whitewashed picket fence complete this charming residence.

The color is at once complex and natural. It is the color of Mother Earth, essentially ocher, which is associated with substance and stability. Variations in light transform this golden ocher into shades of cinnamon, honey, and ecru. The home emits a sense of simplicity, comfort, hearth, and family roots.

All year around, this house just glows. Keep accompanying landscape colors subdued—primarily green foliage and white blossoms. Brick and stone create an even more grounded and ordered look.

Housebody color:	1. Benjamin Moore—Dorset Gold HC-8
Trim:	2. Benjamin Moore—White
Details:	3. Benjamin Moore—Heritage Red 25 on chimney; Benjamin Moore—White on fence

For a Different Look

Try a lovely dark burgundy color on the doors. Make it a deep purple-red. This adds depth and richness to the existing color scheme.

Farmhouse Yellow Medium Lemon Yellow

One day in the country is worth a month in town. —Christina Rossetti

Spring is beautiful in New England. This soft yellow farmhouse casts a warm glow and lives harmoniously in nature. The basic palette is yellow on the house accompanied by an old peeling red on the barn. Notice the green roof, which contributes to the sense of balance, as red is green's complement.

Whether or not your roof is green, consider farmhouse yellow for your clapboard house. It shines within its surroundings and has a hearty quality that sustains its appearance through the chilly depths of winter. Landscape colors may be chosen freely because this palette is so neutral. This color is a classic. Keep the promise of spring alive with this yellow choice.

Housebody color:	1. Benjamin Moore—Light Yellow 2022-60
Trim color:	2. Benjamin Moore—White Dove
Details:	Benjamin Moore—White Dove on doors

For a Different Look

For an uplifting appearance, paint the doors blue—either a light or dark shade. Blue doors will connect the house its surroundings—a vast blue sky. As an alternative to blue, green doors make a nice but more traditional statement.

Perfectly Painted:

Lighter paint colors give a more reflective, brighter appearance.

Housebody color:	1. Sherwin-Williams—Yellow Corn SW2348
Trim color:	2. Sherwin-Williams—Chicory SW2035
Details:	Sherwin-Williams—Chicory SW2035 on door

For a Different Look

Blue is a beautiful color choice for the trim and doors of this adobe, either the blue color of twilight—a pale periwinkle—or a deep azure, midnight blue. A blue with an electric quality is always enlivening.

Adobe Yellow

Ocher

The earth is an Indian thing. —Jack Kerouac

It is no surprise that this golden ocher yellow has special significance in many cultures as symbolic of the sun. In Japan, it is considered the color of heaven.

The color alone gives this house a strong presence. Here, it is offset by the brickwork and brown beams. In the Southwest, where these warm hues predominate, you can add bright orange, cobalt blue, or purple as a trim color, but you can use this yellow in any part of the country on stucco surfaces. If your region doesn't warrant contrasting bright colors as part of the house color scheme, introduce additional colors in planters or within the landscaping. This will provide a stunning embellishment to the house color. Notice the power of black on details such as ironwork. Ocher and black seem meant for each other.

Perfectly Painted:

To highlight the brick front of a house, use a contrasting color such as yellow on the housebody or on details such as shutters.

Deep Gold

This home in the New England vernacular, with its elegant symmetry, is saturated in thick layers of earthy yellow paint. When applying a bold color, confidence is everything. Unfortunately, risk is an essential element in this often anxiety-provoking process. But looking at the rich facade of this old house, you realize the risk is worthwhile. This heavy color cries out for lightness to provide balance. In the absence of additional colors on the housebody, the white picket fencing is the brightening solution. The sparkling white frames the yard and home.

Gold, the color of changing foliage, provides warmth in winter and sunshine in the spring. Your house need not be a historic landmark to be outfitted in this palette. However, architectural simplicity that lets the color be the star is best.

Freely add color within the landscape. You don't need to limit yourself to green.

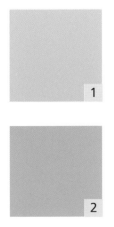

Housebody colors:	1. Benjamin Moore—Roasted Sesame Seed 2160-40
Trim colors:	Benjamin Moore—Buttercup 2154-30
Details:	2. Benjamin Moore—Acadia White AC-41 on window sashes

For a Different Look
To brighten this yellow house, paint the door white. Or, for a more sedate look, paint the door black.

Yellow Detailing

Do you love yellow but worry about painting the whole house? You can get the warmth and friendliness of yellow by incorporating it into paneled carvings and architectural elements such as pillars, trim, or doors. Here are a few examples to consider.

Left:
Yellow is a splendid choice for highlighting the many wonderful details on this blue Victorian. It emits a friendly, happy, even playful mood. Yellow helps make the house more cheerful and warm, too. Accompanying white trim frames the house and draws people in. The addition of this white trim helps to lighten the heft of the house. Yellow and blue alone would create a heavier look.

Opposite, top:
Sunny yellow trim adds warmth and light to the front porch of this Queen Anne row house. Because yellow is a high-reflection color, it advances to the eye, making it a stand-out trim color for any house whose features or lines you would like to accentuate. It would not be the best color choice for a home without details you wish to highlight.

Right:
This carved wooden door detail is truly
enhanced with the simple addition of
gold-leaf paint. The fan shape, with its
glimmering golden rays, gives the whole
house a real lift. This is a very easy way to
bring a sparkle to your home. Treat the
details on your front door with a highlighting color. Even if the entire house and
door are painted the same color, you can
still add personality and a warm welcome
with a splash of golden yellow.

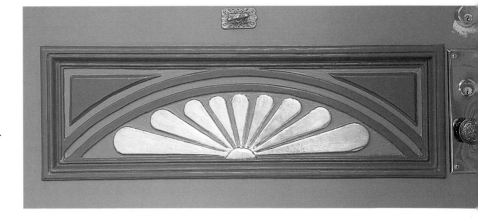

It's not that easy bein' green.

—Joe Raposo, "Bein' Green," sung by Kermit the Frog

It's true; green is not the most popular exterior paint color. You may be hesitant to paint your house green for fear that it will look like a giant lime or a Crayola crayon. But don't worry. This section will change the way you think about green. These recipes are tried and true.

Nature put more greens on earth than any other color—thousands of variations on emerald, chartreuse, pine, sage, and olive. Green is about renewal, hope, life, and fertility.

Consider giving your home a new life with seafoam, a soft, pale green perfect in both northern and southern climates, and trimming it in cream. The palest tints of blue-green, such as aquamarine and turquoise, evoke distant images of the placid Aegean Sea. Moss-green siding is perfect with crisp white window frames.

Want a dramatic change? Decorate your red brick house with a wintergreen door, shutters, and window boxes. Or paint the accent moldings of your weathered shingle house in vibrant green and sunny yellow to completely brighten and freshen the look.

If you are inclined to paint your house green, chances are you are a stable, balanced, social person. Enjoy entertaining in a home wrapped in nature's most popular hue.

The Frog Prince Bright Emerald

The eye experiences a distinctly grateful impression from

this color. —Goethe

Modest Victorian houses of no distinct style are found across the country. This bright green house, with its crisp white trim, does not reflect nineteenth-century painting practices. It was not customary to paint the entire house one color, nor to have the cornice, corner boards, and window and door frames in stark contrast. However, the choice of this particular green was the perfect way to turn this frog into a prince. This green has a clean, fresh quality that shines within the surrounding landscape.

Though simple, this house is a color showstopper. Green might be a wonderful color choice for your Victorian home too. You can avoid clashing with this green by landscaping with yellow.

Housebody color:	1. Benjamin Moore—Cedar Green 2034-40
Trim and door color:	2. Benjamin Moore—Brilliant White

For a Different Look
A pale yellow on the front door would make this house more brilliant, sunny, and warm. For even more color, use the same yellow (as well as white) in the carved designs, on the window frames, and along the eaves.

Eternally Green Deep Blue-Green

On a gray day it will look like a moth; on a sunny day like a butterfly. —Louis I. Kahn

The strength of this contemporary mission-style bungalow lies in its choice of building materials, its geometry, and its paint colors. Its style is rendered less common by unusual choices—in color, of deep blue-green, and of varying sizes of clapboards, shingles, and heavy concrete columns. Varnished wooden window frames take on an orange glow and brighten the serious edge of a rather somber green house.

Charcoal-gray detailing complements the cream-colored patio and architectural elements and introduces yet another color. The house feels grounded and earthy, yet is enlivened with multiple details.

This blue-green is unobtrusive. It blends well with the outdoor environment and is an especially handsome choice. It combines color qualities of the sky and of the foliage and doesn't compete with either. Green is the most restful color to the eye.

To enliven your surroundings, landscape with lots of color—yellow iris, purple pansies, pink azaleas, orange daylilies and marigolds, and white bleeding heart.

1 | 2 | 3

Housebody color:	1. Benjamin Moore—Casco Bay 2051-30
Trim color:	2. Benjamin Moore—Witching Hour 2120-30
Details:	3. Benjamin Moore—Moonlight White 2143-60 on columns; orange-tone stain and varnish on window frames

For a Different Look

For a smashing effect, try a deep cobalt blue on the doors. It is more dramatic than the existing green and gives the house a dreamy quality. Paint all the window frames pumpkin orange.

Camp House

Forest Green

To invite a person into your house is to take charge of his happiness for as long as he is under your roof. —Anthelme Brillat-Savarin

This forest green reminds me of the great outdoors. It has a strong and stable quality, much like the tall pines surrounding it. Charming and casual, the house has a laid-back kind of elegance.

Green is known as the great harmonizer by Indian mystics, to whom it represents the balance and harmony found in nature. This house, with its green color, does convey a sense of calm and of balance. Although it is dark, the color is still neutral and subtle.

The color chosen for this house allows a large, expensive home to take on an air of modesty—a camp quality. The house, its surroundings, and its colors are strangely dramatic in their serenity.

Landscaping should be done as though nature did it herself.

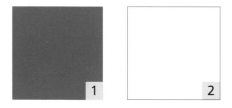

Housebody color: 1. Sherwin Williams—Mown Grass SW 2377

Trim color: 2. Sherwin Williams—White SW 2123

For a Different Look
Try incorporating more color into this scheme. Simply paint the door a lovely silvery, blueberry blue. The added interest will amaze you.

Perfectly Painted:

To make a house blend into its surroundings, avoid colors that contrast with those surroundings.

Victorian Sage Pale, Silvery Gray-Green

My salad days, when I was green in judgment.

—William Shakespeare, *Antony and Cleopatra*

This pale, silvery gray-green reminds me of the lovely shimmering perennial called lamb's ear. It has a soft and delicate quality. Overall, the house has a neutral, sophisticated, subtle color palette that emits a sort of luminescence. The palest green is strengthened with darker green and gray and highlighted with white trim. Wooden gingerbread fretwork brings a jaunty quality to this house, an air of frivolity.

Your house may not have this much detailing. It may not even be a Victorian, but that doesn't mean you can't accentuate its positives using these colors. Green is the primary color, with white for detailing. Throw in a pinch of violet (as here, on the stained glass windows) for fun.

A large blossoming tree in green's complementary color (red) balances out the home perfectly.

Housebody color:	1. California Paints Historic Color— Glenhaven 8134M
Trim color:	2. California Paints—Beach Basket 7750W
Details:	3. California Paints—Shaded Moss 8136N

For a Different Look

How about adding a pale violet-blue door? This color of lilac blossoms combined with the green house body color is reminiscent of the fresh colors of spring.

Green Detailing

Do you love green but worry about painting the whole house? You can get the pleasure of green even if you use it only sparingly on the doors or the detailing. Here are just a few examples.

Below:
Most greens are associated with the earth as the color of vegetation. But blue-green is more closely associated with the cool, refreshing ocean. On this building, blue-green is unobtrusive, blending in with the outdoor environment. It doesn't compete with the landscape, yet it adds a slight sparkle to its restful surroundings. If your goal is to create a sophisticated, upscale, soothing and fresh look for your house with only a splash of color, try blue-green.

Above:
There is an enormous range of green colors. This green is similar to the greens found in nature. In choosing this color, the house immediately becomes linked to its surroundings. Even with green trim, this house is neutral, because green is nature's neutral—the colors of foliage and growing plants. Green brings a sense of balance and harmony to this home.

Blue

...[A]s readily as we follow

an agreeable object that flies from us so we love to contemplate

blue, not because it advances to us, but because it draws us

after it. —Goethe, *Theory of Colors*

Blue is America's favorite color. Perhaps this is because blue suggests images of the sky and the sea, vast and serene. In truth, the brain's response to blue is relaxation. If you are contemplating painting your house blue, chances are it has always been your favorite color. You probably aspire to harmony, peace, perseverance, patience, and tranquility.

Blue is a dependable choice. Blue houses create a sense of coolness on a hot summer day and a rich, welcome contrast to white winter snow. Autumn provides the perfect complement (orange) to a blue domain.

Pale or light blue houses, like powder blue and Wedgwood blue, feel retiring, quiet and soothing, while deeper indigo blues, like cobalt and marine, come alive to offer a dramatic contrast to nature's colors. Flower-filled beds and bushes with blooms are even lovelier against the richness and timelessness of glorious blue.

Vivid indigo or cornflower blue houses make bold statements when paired with tangerine-orange or lime-green doors. For a traditional look, try black on the shutters and white on all the trim, or select a soft blue with off-white trim and yellow shutters for a more country feel. Pale blue shutters on a deeper blue house work well when coupled with black window frames and door. Change the look of stucco instantly with vivid azure blue accents. Aqua makes tan stucco look polished rather than drab. Blue houses seem to soar skyward, for they have a celestial quality. Enjoy the range of blue choices in these recipes.

Perfectly Painted:

Subtler colors can be emphasized by using their complement

or analogous colors on shutters, doors, etc. (see Appendix A).

Country Blue

Pale Blue-Gray

If you love me (but not quite),

Send me a ribbon, a ribbon of white.

If you love me, love me true,

Send me a ribbon, a ribbon of blue. —Nursery rhyme

Pale blue adds interest and charm to this country house, particularly because it is nestled between many white houses. Crisp white trim, red doors, and pale gray shutters give the house a neat and tidy finish. The house is accentuated by the emerald lawn in the foreground and the accompanying colorful palette of flowers.

This lovely paint treatment works as well on clapboard as it does on shake and shingles. Consider including lush greenery and adding brilliance with colorful flowers. Multicolored and white blossoms, especially reds, pinks, and purples, can be planted in profusion.

Unembellished homes can often be made to have as much presence as houses with applied decoration simply with paint.

This paint color suggests a sense of peace and tranquility.

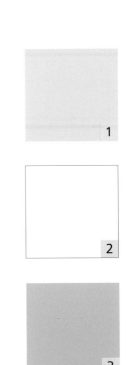

Housebody color:	1. Sherwin-Williams—Skyway Blue SW2263
Trim color:	2. Sherwin-Williams White
Details:	3. Sherwin-Williams—Canal Blue SW2261 on shutters
	4. Sherwin-Williams—Elderberry SW 2902 on doors

For a Different Look

How about a pink door? It doesn't have to be bright pink. It can be a subtle, grayed pink. The color would be an uplifting, friendly addition to this blue house. Consider substituting blue shutters for the existing gray shutters. Find a fairly deep shade of blue that appeals to you. This color combination will transform your traditional house to a quaint and charming home with a touch of whimsy.

Slate Dark Slate Blue

A man possessed by peace never stops smiling. —Milan Kundera

Here is a stunning example of the enormous impression a dark color can make on the appearance of a house. This historic blue home appears formal and serious, tranquil and peaceful. Imagine if this house were painted all white, or a light color. It would present an altogether completely different mood for the viewer.

Notice that the trim is painted the same color as the house. With so little color contrast, the house feels stayed and grounded. A burgundy door provides the only break in color and adds some warmth. A short, delicate white fence lightens the heaviness of the house.

If you like dark, historic colors, and your clapboard house has simple, straightforward lines without a lot of detailing, you may be able to use this recipe. Keep your landscaping low. You can certainly add more color within your plantings. Notice the impact of the light wisps of pale-colored perennials and consider adding them into your landscape.

Housebody color: 1. Benjamin Moore—Hamilton Blue 36

Trim color: Benjamin Moore—Hamilton Blue 36

Details: 2. Benjamin Moore—Cherokee Brick 2082-30

For a Different Look

Consider a black door rather than a burgundy red door. It will not change the character of the house. Rather, it makes an already well-groomed home appear even more formal.

Perfectly Painted:

Dark paint colors don't show dirt as easily as light colors do.

Perfectly Painted:

Use a contrasting color to paint around the outside edge of all the window and door frames to create visual interest and unify the overall design.

Gloucester Victorian Blue-Gray

Come in the evening, come in the morning. Come when expected, come without warning; Thousands of welcomes you'll find here before you, and the oftener you come, the more we'll adore you. —Irish rhyme

Check out the interesting combination of blues on this unusual Victorian house. Blue-gray clapboards are toned down by the slightly more intense blue door and window sashes. A bravura splash of warm yellow trim and gold detailing creates an eye-popping contrast and makes the blue on the house feel as cool as a cucumber.

Can you use these colors on your house? Yes, easily. Simply apply the colors to your ranch house, bungalow, cape or beach house. Blue-gray is great on clapboards, but also works on shingles and even on stucco. Gold can be used as an accent color on wooden house details.

The vivid colors used on the house, and its inherent architectural interest, make a strong statement without the need for any major landscaping. A few low-growing greens and pretty annuals or perennials will add softness to the hard lines of the architecture. Keep the look casual, perhaps in the style of a cottage garden.

Housebody color:	1. Benjamin Moore Historic Colors—Whipple Blue HC-152
Trim color:	2. Benjamin Moore—Hepplewhite Ivory HC-36
Details:	3. Benjamin Moore—Deep Ocean 2058-30 on doors and window sashes
	4. Benjamin Moore—Chestertown Buff HC-9 on wooden details

For a Different Look

Try using the existing colors in this recipe, but on different parts of the house. For instance, you could use the house body color on the window sashes. This allows you to emphasize the colors you want without changing the color scheme or stylistic details. Consider using a different color on the doors. Red or gold are great options.

Pale Blue-Gray Cottage

There are fairies at the bottom of our garden!

—Rose Fyleman

This lovely blue bungalow house is illuminated by the May morning sun. It glows during daytime hours and, in the evening, seems almost to vibrate with color, giving the house a magical quality. Its Gothic windows and deeper blue trim heighten the effect. Gentle white dogwood blossoms and natural splashes of violet azalea and rhododendron enliven it further. This color is alive, yet calming. Green foliage provides a lush surrounding and ties the dreamlike house to reality.

If you love blue and have a shingled, stucco, or clapboard cape, ranch, or bungalow, this may be just the color palette for you. It is enchanting without being shocking or overly fanciful. This is a color that demands special attention. Your house will surely draw interest, having an aura of mystery and intrigue.

Housebody color:	1. California Paints—Basin Blue 7991W
Trim color:	2. California Paints—Wonder Blue 7524M
Details:	California Paints—Ocean Depths 8045D on inner windows

For a Different Look
Paint the front door white instead of blue—it will contemporize the house and give it a clean fresh look.

Blue Detailing

Do you love blue but worry about painting the whole house? Bring the serenity of blue into your color scheme by painting only the shutters, trim, doors, or other house details. Here are a couple of examples.

Left:
What a knockout this charcoal house becomes with a cobalt blue door. With or without the bright yellow window trim, this house is awakened with cobalt blue. Vivid, brilliant blue is electrifying. It energizes the entire house and lends a welcoming, playful quality. Deeper blues have a meditative quality making it the perfect blue choice for this house set among tall pines in the forest.

Above:

Blue shutters add not merely color to this lovely Cape but create a mood of tranquility. The house seems to have a consoling spirit—not surprising since blue is felt to be a spiritually calming color. Gazing at this house produces a sense of contentment and relaxation. If you wish to create a peaceful, serene atmosphere, choose blue as your shutter color—and use it on the front door too.

The purest and most thoughtful

minds are those which love color the most. —John Ruskin

Whether a delicate mauve or deep plum, violet is sophisticated and can be highly successful as a house paint color.

We tend to think of violet as exotic because it was once the color reserved for royalty and is still the color of exotic blossoms and fruits. But violets come in an exciting array of shades from casual to chic. All are combinations of the primary colors blue and red.

Violet is generally considered a cool color. The bluer the violet, the more subdued, tranquil, and cool the color appears. The redder the violet, the more it advances to the eye and takes on red's stimulating, hot qualities. So, when you choose among violets, think in terms of its red or blue undertones as well as its lightness and brightness to achieve your desired effect. You will enjoy the character of lavender, plum, grape, opal, dark aubergine, and orchid and the wonders they work in sunlight.

Picture a run-of-the-mill house made distinctive with dusty purple-gray paint and parrot-green shutters. This bit of whimsy adds the necessary charm to make the house the quaintest on the street.

For a subtler look, try a blue-gray violet on the body of the house and cream and gray on trim and windows. This is a soft, clean look that freshens, brightens, and updates even the dingiest old house. It makes a bright backdrop for evergreen bushes, climbing vines, and beds of annuals or perennials.

If you love violet, you are probably highly creative, artistic, and sensitive as well as generous and charming. You aren't afraid to be different. The recipes that follow are chosen for folks from shy to adventurous.

Indigo

Here is a fearless paint color for you—a bright lilac purple. It brings this bungalow to life and draws us in. The house is punctuated by white trim and hints of yellow coreopsis.

With this paint color, an otherwise ordinary house becomes a cool oasis. If you dare to be bold and paint your house lilac purple, violet paint with white trim is all you really need. Notice that the porch balusters are painted in accents of blue for consistency and simplicity. Add dashes of color within the landscape.

Notice how the fixed features are neutral—cement walk, weathered wood fence. Thus, the house is truly the point of interest. You have the option of using green or red trim rather than white. These alternatives will work well but generate a camp or cabinlike feeling.

  1  2  3 4

Housebody color:	1. Benjamin Moore—California Lilac 2068-40
Trim color:	2. Benjamin Moore—Brilliant White
Details:	3. Benjamin Moore—Bermuda Blue 2061-30
	4. Benjamin Moore—Dior Gray 2133-40

For a Different Look

Consider the use of green or red trim rather than white for a cabin-like feel. Or, use all the designated colors indicated in the recipe except the door color. Instead, paint the door red. This makes an already bold statement even more dynamic.

Regal Violet

Soothing Grape

Mid pleasures and palaces though we may roam,

Be it ever so humble, there's no place like home.

—J. Howard Payne, *Clari, the Maid of Milan*

This grape-colored Victorian is representative of the row-house style, seen from down the Mississippi, across the lower South, up the East Coast to New England, back to the Midwest, and out to the Rockies and the California coast, where it has gained much fame.

The soothing, lovely grape color and accompanying cobalt trim, combined with creamy off-white, gray-green, and violet detailing create an elegantly eclectic color mixture. The balanced facade is accentuated by the detailing on the portico pilasters, porch, and door. This is a stunning example of the regal quality that emanates from some tones of purple. The majestic, rich, interesting, and sophisticated quality of this home is due, in part, to its inherent architectural beauty, but also to the choices in paint colors.

Be careful with your selection of landscape colors. Simple evergreen foundation plantings with one or two potted flowers on the portico is all you really need.

Housebody color:	1. Benjamin Moore—Gentle Violet 2071-20
Trim:	2. Benjamin Moore—Navajo White
Details:	3. Benjamin Moore—Twilight Blue 2067-30 on trim;
	4. Benjamin Moore—Misty Lilac 2071-70;
	5. Benjamin Moore—Northampton Putty HC-89 on porch and door

For a Different Look
Simply use white paint on the porch and door for a lighter, crisper look.

Perfectly Painted:

Columns or pillars can be painted with one main color and up to three accent colors on carved parts.

Gillman Garrison House Plum

He best can paint them who shall feel them most.

—Alexander Pope

The color purple makes an exciting and memorable impact on the unpretentious honesty of a simple Colonial wood house. The Gillman Garrison House (c. 1690) was originally built as a fortified house to protect local sawmills. Who would guess? This New England house keeps its secrets behind plum-colored clapboards. A pale brown natural wooden door and white trim highlight the few ornamental moldings and doorways. The subtle purple and pink undertones in the red brick walk tie into the house color.

Purple is a wonderful and unusual color choice. Why settle for brown or even red when you can have this sophisticated, colorful plum? Does your home have simple, clean lines with few or no embellishments? Do you enjoy the minimalist look? These are the main criteria for using this paint color. The color itself provides all the interest you will need. It even negates the need to accessorize. Purple intrigues the eye in every landscape. Try it and see.

Housebody Color:	1. California Paints—Glorious Plum 8905D
Trim Color:	2. California Paints—White Solitude CW057W
Details:	Natural wood stained doors

For a Different Look

Some people prefer a painted front door. Think about the colors that you like, and then consider how they might work with purple. For instance, barn or cherry reds may not work well for you on this purple house. Black works with almost all colors. Green is great with purple. Some blues also work with purple. Orange would be extremely dramatic and bold. Experiment, and find your favorite.

Violet Detailing

Do you love violet but worry about painting the whole house? You can get added color interest using your creative touch and violet even if it is applied only to the doors, trim, or on other house details. Here are some wonderful examples.

Right:
Heather-toned violet-blue details cool down this yellow house and add a hint of refinement. It is a quiet and low-key color, making it a nice, serene choice for embellishing your Victorian.

Opposite, top:
Do you love violet but prefer not to paint it on the house? Then plant a wisteria and drape the entire front of your house in violet. The plant becomes a fixed feature on the house adding drama, character, and color during part of each year. Make a chocolate brown house extraordinary with masses of violet blossoms.

Right:
This whimsical, witty combination of accent colors brings a unique character to this little house. And, since people who prefer violet tend to be artists and nonconformists, it's no wonder that violet dominates the scheme. Included are a light and darker violet, with its complement, yellow, and a high impact berry red. The result is a wonderful combination of excitement and tranquility.

Violet is viewed by mystics as the color of spiritual intuition. Perhaps it was chosen for this reason, because in this landscape, the house seems to take on something of a mystical quality.

White, Gray, Brown

... possess a sturdiness, a strong powerfulness which is not immediately evident. —B. J. Koumer, *Color Their Characters*

The word *neutral* is misleading because neutral colors run the gamut from pale tans, creams, and beige that only hint at color to deep umber browns, nutmegs, and dark gray. The range of color within the neutral spectrum is tremendous. Think of the difference between ivory and charcoal. Neutrals are elegant when contrasted with one another. White, brown, and black all exhibit both warmth and coolness depending on their companion or surrounding colors. They can be used with great success alongside bright or exotic colors, such as shocking pink or azure blue.

White

White is probably America's most common house color. Its popularity began in the Greek Revival era (c. 1830 – 1855) because of the mistaken impression that ancient Greeks lived in white buildings. (Golden Age Greek buildings were, in fact, bright and colorful.) Brilliant whites often have blue pigment added and are so bright they actually appear cool. Ivory, bone, parchment, and other off-whites are warmer choices. White reflects the light of the sunshine and the colors of its surroundings—the grass, the sky. White houses can be traditional or playful, depending on your use of colored trim and the style of your house. Imagine a white house with bright green trim the color of spring grass. Or red shutters and blue and white striped awnings for a nautical look. How about a white brick house with red trim and doors? A cream house with gray trim and a bright red-orange door has a stately look and a brilliantly welcoming entry. A combination of white and off-white is subtle but lively.

If you love white houses, you are probably neat and orderly. White shows form to its greatest advantage and is, therefore, great on contemporary homes, featuring their lines against grass and sky.

Gray

Gray is always a popular house paint color choice. It is nature's most perfect neutral and works well with every color of the rainbow. When placed next to another color, gray assumes a bit of that color's complement. Gray beside green seems slightly rosy. Gray beside orange takes on a bit of blue. Keep this in mind as you select trim and accent colors. Gray is especially wonderful on shingled houses, on clapboard homes, and for an old, weathered look. Gray-tinted stucco is pleasant. Whether charcoal, pearly, silvery, smoky, or pale, gray is dignified and conservative. Gray has a long-standing association with stone and rock—solid and strong. If you love gray, you are probably practical, calm, composed, and reliable.

Brown

Brown is down to earth, understated, rugged, and outdoorsy. It comes in a wide variety of popular choices for exteriors: brown sugar, coffee, cocoa, chocolate, cinnamon, light browns (like beige and tan), and taupe browns (gray-browns). Brown is a classic color. It is always understated and dignified. Picture Boston's brownstones and the Southwest's adobe brick houses. Brown is the perfect background for lively touches of color like red, blue, green, and white, which cheer its serious character. People who think they don't like brown often do love brown wood furnishings and floors. If you don't want a brown house, consider the lovely natural tones of a wood door. Those who favor brown have a down-to-earth love of simplicity and a reliable character.

Enjoy the colorful neutral recipes. You are sure to find one for your home sweet home.

Glowing
Gray Medium-Pale Putty Gray

Every branch big with it,

Bent every twig with it;

Every fork like a white web-foot;

Every street and pavement mute:

Some flakes have lost their way, and grope back upward, when

Meeting those meandering down they turn and descend again.

The palings are glued together like a wall,

And there is no waft of wind with the fleecy fall.

—Thomas Hardy, "Snow in the Suburbs"

Your doorbell rings. You open the door to the sounds of carolers dressed in colorful Christmas clothes, all bundled up in fuzzy hats, scarves, and mittens. There are children wearing wreaths of stars around their heads. It is a picture-perfect photo opportunity depicting *Home for the Holidays*. However, you don't need to live in snow country to enjoy this paint color recipe.

Every shade of gray is slightly different because each contains particles of many other colors. This putty gray is particularly stunning in winter, appearing luminous and glowing. The drama is created by pairing medium-pale gray with deeper gray shutters and contrasting it with white trim. House features become elegant silhouettes that attract the eye. For a greater sense of drama and formality, you can paint shutters black and consider a black door as well. While especially lovely in winter, this house has a depth and presence at any time of the year. Elegant, homey, and serene, this lovely gray and white color combination is a winning choice.

Housebody color:	1. California Paints—Phelps Putty
Trim color:	2. California Paints—Nu-White 4-7100
Details:	3. California Paints—Fieldstone on shutters

For a Different Look

There are a wide variety of grays that you might like on your shutters ranging from pewter tones to gray-greens. Don't feel limited by the gray provided with this recipe. Very deep green, almost black, is also a great shutter color on this gray house. A black door makes the classic accompaniment.

Gothic Beige Gray and Brown

As fair as morn, as fresh as May... —from a madrigal by John Wilbye

This gray and rosy-brown Gothic cottage with its natural stained wood door is elegant and warm. During the nineteenth century, the trim color would have been painted significantly darker than the house. Now, many homeowners prefer a subtler, smoother transition in color between the house and trim that is easier on the eye. For this reason, we often see white or off-white trim on these homes today, as evidenced here by the white trim detailing on the gable. Historically accurate colors are often viewed as too dark or drab and hold little appeal for today's homeowners.

This simple yet sophisticated palette looks equally as appealing on a Colonial Revival and on any of the smaller houses of the 1950s and 1960s—the split levels, ranches, and capes typically found in subdivisions. The color combination is effective on clapboard, shingle, and stucco houses as well. Any home with a cottage quality will look lovely in these colors. If you love the gray house body color, but not the rosey-brown trim, feel free to substitute it with a green or a violet color. Both alternative trim colors will change the mood of the house from warm to cool.

Foundation plantings are green with splashes of violet azalea and white hydrangea. Pale brick walks are completely neutral.

Perfectly Painted:

If you are choosing from neutral colors (white, grey, black or brown), consider the other color tones within the chosen color. For example, if you plan to paint your house brown, determine if it is gray-brown, red-brown, gold-brown, and so on. This will help you pick appropriate paint colors for the detail and trim colors. Specifically, use colors that are analogous to your color scheme (see Appendix A).

Housebody colors:	1. Benjamin Moore—Pink Beige SW2018
Trim colors:	2. Sherwin-Williams—Kashmir Sand SW2282
Details:	Natural wood door

For a Different Look
Violet-gray or green are great alternatives as door and trim colors.

White with a Twist

White, Cobalt Blue, and Yellow

Blow trumpet, for the world is white with May. —Alfred, Lord Tennyson

This white house is anything but neutral, with its yellow stars and blue shutters. The main house is plain white. Added to it are two tones of yellow and blue. What a stunning result! Granted, this house is an architectural jewel, but your white house can become something special too with colored detailing.

White houses are distinguished by their ability to reflect light. If you choose to paint your house white, why settle for traditional black or dark green shutters? Switch from prim to playful. While vibrant colors often do cause people to shy away in fear of making a color mistake, remember, it is just paint and can be easily altered. Try something dynamic—but be sure to test the colors on the house yourself before giving your painter the green light.

Don't let color scare you. For example, on a simple center-front Colonial, you could use blue on the shutters and two tones of yellow on a paneled front door. You would eliminate the natural wood all together. Or, perhaps, you have a Victorian. In this, case your options for color placement are numerable. Incorporate all of these colors within your scheme, making your favorite colors among them the most prominent.

Choose your favorite colors for flowers and landscaping. Anything goes here. Try simple evergreens with a hint of color or go all out with a multicolored planting palette. Keep the theme simple or go wild with perennial blooms.

Housebody and trim color: 1. Pittsburgh Paints—Super White 88-45

Details: 2. Pittsburgh Paints—Overcast 249-4 on shutters
3. Pittsburgh Paints—Chickadee 113-5

For a Different Look

Try an even brighter blue on the doors and shutters, such as a deep cobalt or azure blue. This look will be more striking and bold. If blue is not your color, red is a suitable bold alternative to blue.

Taupe
Beauty Gray-Brown, Taupe

I specialize in prying pearls from oysters.

—Philip Tilden, on remodeling large old houses

Brown is a classic color. It has a timeless, dependable appearance. This gray-brown almost looks like fine suede. Brown is easy to live with. It has a chameleonlike quality and seems to take on shades of the colors surrounding it. The many variations of undertone make taupe a favorite neutral to serve as a subtle background for elaborate displays of color, like those in this garden. The fantastic array of perennials and annuals and the lush trees more than compensate for potential blandness in the house color. The outcome is luxurious, subtle, and understated.

Brown need never be drab or dull, nor must it lead to a lack of visual stimulation. Simply choose the right brown, like this delicious, rich taupe, and go wild with lively landscape colors. Fancy window frames and a dash of golden yellow on doors are the main details on this Victorian.

But taupe is also suited to many other architectural styles. Imagine the clean, soft look of a fresh taupe coat on formerly tired siding. The subtlety of taupe lets the garden take center stage in this color scheme.

1

2

3

Housebody color:	1. Benjamin Moore—Dusty Ranch Brown 2105-40
Trim color:	2. Benjamin Moore—White
Details:	3. Benjamin Moore—Pearl Harbor 2165-50 on door panels

For a Different Look

Substitute the gold details on this house with your favorite shade of deep blue or berry red. Both of these colors are more colorful than the existing gold, but have a less earthy, prettier quality.

Golden Straw Beige-Brown

Things are seldom what they seem,

Skim milk masquerades as cream.

—W. S. Gilbert, *H.M.S. Pinafore*

Brown, when seen in wood tones, is so neutral that it is not often thought of as a color at all. Even people who express a dislike for brown often unconsciously surround themselves with wood floors and wood furnishings. This beige-brown, the lightest of earth tones, is soft, wholesome, and unpretentious. It has the glowing warmth of wheat fields.

A color enthusiast may think a brown house is out of the question—but look at this example. This home is beautiful without a shred of landscaping or even a wink of color. The stained wood blends in gently with the forest behind it. What a stunning effect! To achieve this look, you must start with new clapboard and stain it. White trim frames the house. If this is too neutral for your taste, the front door is the most logical place to display color.

A deep plum or crimson red on the door would give a neutral house more personality and make it stand out from the surrounding landscape. Let your door color choice be a reflection of you. Or, use a natural wooden door, such as oak, that is a darker tone than the clapboard. This will add an element of color without using paint, and maintain the rustic appeal of the house body color.

Housebody color: 1. Benjamin Moore Moorewood Siding Stains—Desert Sand

Trim color and details: 2. Benjamin Moore—White

For a Different Look

Treat the doors to a deep plum, midnight blue, or crimson red. This will provide some color to the house without altering its earthy simplicity.

Neutral Detailing

You want your home neutral and subtle but still want it noticed?
Try adding only elements of color.

Opposite, top:
Red, more than any other color, elicits strong emotions. It is interesting that red was chosen as the accent color for this neutral, charcoal colored barn. The owner must have intended his viewer to experience an emotional reaction to the barn. It sits in a tranquil environment and would probably go completely unnoticed if it weren't for its red cupola that provides strong contrast against the sky and demands your attention. For a blast of impact, add a dash of red to your home—perhaps on your front door.

Opposite, bottom:
Here is another example of a neutral house that gets its color interest from a contrasting colored natural wooden door. The wood tones have a golden-yellow glow, particularly under incandescent light at night. The brown roof shingles have strong red undertones. Both of these fixed features—the door and the roof—provide significant contrast to the neutral grays and browns of the house body. Paint color need not be used to achieve color contrast.

Above:
An old oak door is all that is needed to provide color contrast to this dark wooden and pale stucco house. Tones of red, yellow, and gold become readily apparent on the door when viewed within the context of the house. The door, while substantial in heft, actually seems to lighten the heaviness of the house merely with its lighter color. If you want contrast, you don't necessarily need to use paint color to get it. Wood has so many colorful overtones that it may be the solution for you. Natural wood is especially pleasing on doors, porches, and garage doors.

Doorways

Create enormous impact for your point of entry with colors from the Glidden Company. These identical houses are pictured with various color differences. Each façade has a distinctly different look or mood. Create the mood of your choice for your house by considering its doorway colors.

Earthy tones are used on the house, trim, and windows to make a color scheme that echoes the natural materials found in the landscape. When you combine the colors of stone and wood, the result is a low-key, easy-going welcome.

CALM

CLAPBOARD	TRIM	WINDOWS
Stone Harbor	Great Smokie Mt.	Turret Brown
(10YY 48/071)	(00YY 19/068)	(80YR 17/129)

FRESH

CLAPBOARD	TRIM	WINDOWS
Brittany Inn	White Wing	Aberdeen Place
(70BG 31/124)	(50GY 83/010)	(70RR 08/150)

Red windows, door trim, and banisters bring a real zing to the entrance of this blue house. A nice, striking contrast is created between the house color and trim colors by framing them all in white. The architectural elements of the house are accented. The colors strike a balance between cool and hot, which gives the house a lot of personality.

WARM

CLAPBOARD	TRIM	WINDOWS
Antique Linen	Stowe White	Afternoon Tea
(30YY 70/120)	(45YY 83/062)	(80YR 21/226)

The simplicity of this look is very appealing. Crisp white trim brightens the warm, pale beige house. It is inviting and cheerful.

VIBRANT

CLAPBOARD	TRIM	WINDOWS
Dover Grey	Zanzibar Coast	Deep Onyx
(00NN 45/000)	(10YR 10/174)	(00NN 07/000)

Deep, dark brown adds substance and weight to this pale gray house. Several brown paint colors were used for trim, creating interest and dimension. This house has a more majestic look than the other examples pictured here.

Hot red clapboard and a very dark brown door make this house seem heavier than most of the other examples pictured here. The house is grounded in earth colors. Beige trim keeps the contrast between the house and trim minimal. White trim would have had the opposite effect making the house seem to "jump out" at the viewer. This is a warm, earthy facade.

VIBRANT

CLAPBOARD
Old Redwood
(30YR 08/236)

TRIM
Arrow Wood
(10YY 27/060)

DOOR
Manor House
(50YR 08/038)

This very neutral paint color treatment is tranquil and calm. It has an airy, gentle quality. The clapboard is a cool beige. A taupe door adds warmth. This is a pleasant, low-key entrance.

CALM

CLAPBOARD
Archives
(50YR 46/028)

TRIM
White Bucks
(10YY 72/021)

DOOR
Elephant
(50YR 17/029)

Pale blue-gray clapboards and pale gray trim have a sparkling effect on the appearance of this entryway. The colors are soft, cool, and crisp. A chocolate brown door brings warmth and weight to the house. This is a refreshing entryway.

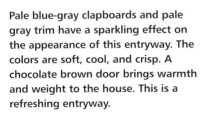

FRESH

CLAPBOARD
Library Hall
(90GG 53/048)

TRIM
Grey Ghost
(50BG 83/004)

DOOR
Rowhouse
(70YR 25/106)

Bright, cheery yellow clapboard makes a welcoming and friendly facade. The door is a cool green that balances the warmth of the yellow. This is an upbeat entrance.

WARM

CLAPBOARD
Portuguese Sonnet
(45YY 65/334)

TRIM
White on White
(30GY 88/014)

SHUTTERS
Pine Grove
(90GY 13/161)

Color Schemes

The traditional approach to choosing a color scheme is to use either a complementary or an analogous scheme.

This simply means that you choose the house color, then determine paint colors for the detailing (trim, eaves, shutters, doors, and so on) in colors that have less contrast (analogous) or more contrast (complementary). Victorian and other nineteenth-century architectural styles had many features that could be highlighted with paint, and many beautifully exemplify complementary schemes. Conversely, many homes have elements that are best allowed to fade into the background. This is where an analogous color scheme is the better choice. But you can consider using paint to accentuate details or to add them where the architecture is plain or where a mood change is desired.

The color wheel displays transitions from color to color and shows their relationships. The colors on the wheel are intense and rarely used without tinting (lightening) or shading (darkening) them with black, gray, or white. The color wheel is a good tool for learning to combine colors effectively.

Analogous colors are next to or near each other on the color wheel and provide the least contrast (e.g., combining blue, blue-gray, and deep blue yields a subtle effect). An analogous scheme can literally be tints and shades of the same color, providing minimal contrast. An example of an analogous scheme is a green landscape with a pale blue house, blue-green window trim and doors, and white for the remaining trim to frame the house.

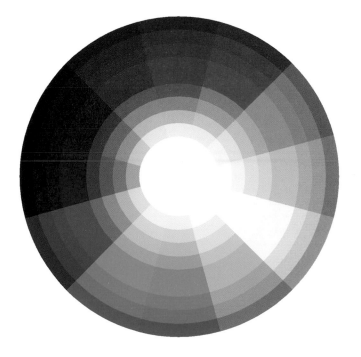

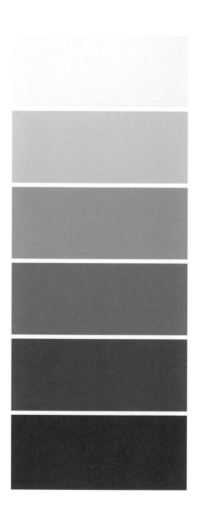

Complementary colors are directly opposite on the color wheel and provide the most dramatic contrast. A green house with a red door represents a complementary scheme. Sometimes a two-color complementary color scheme doesn't offer enough contrast to bring out the interesting details of a house. On Victorian houses, for instance, multiple colors can make the home spectacular. Or picture a Southwestern house with a terra-cotta roof. You can choose a pale tint of yellow-orange for the main house color, a darker shade or yellow-orange for the trim (eaves and fascias), and its complement, a gorgeous blue-purple, for the window trim and doors.

If you desire even more color contrast but want to ensure that the color scheme is balanced, consider these four ways to increase the complementary color palette using more than two colors. Let's take a closer look at our Southwestern house to illustrate.

1. Split complements: Yellow-orange and blue-purple are complements. Choose one for the house color. Now use the two colors adjacent to that color on the color wheel. In this case, where we chose yellow-orange for the house color, the adjacent colors are blue and purple. Consider blue for the window trim and eaves and purple

for the doors.

2. Double complements: Split two complementary colors to their adjacent colors. For example, red is the complement of green. Red-orange and red-purple are the double complements of blue-green and yellow-green.

3. Color triad: Divide colors on the wheel into a triangle. Orange, green, and purple form a triad, as do yellow, blue, and red. Selecting color triads will help to ensure a successful paint color scheme.

4. Mutual complements: Use an analogous scheme plus a complementary color. If the main color is yellow-green, then green and blue-green are the analogous colors. The complement is red, the median value of the analogous colors.

Use either an analogous or complementary scheme to determine your colors. Because you are working with paint, be sure to consider the tints and shades as you see them on the paint strip, not on the color wheel, to select the actual paint colors.

You must also consider the tints and shades—that is, the lightness and darkness of colors. To make it easier to visualize your house colors, consider creating a visual aid.

Creating a Visual Aid

Begin by taking a photograph of your house from across the street as head-on as possible. Take the shot when the house is in complete light or complete shade. Make an 8- x 10-inch (20 cm x 25 cm) print. Lay tracing paper over it. In pencil, outline the house, doors, windows, and trim. Trace outlines of trees or plantings and all fixed features. Keep the drawing simple. Once you are satisfied with your drawing, draw over the pencil lines in ink. Make three or four photocopies.

Color in the photocopies, using crayons, watercolors, or colored pencils, in several color schemes. Use ideas from other homes or magazines, books, and the color wheel. Color the grass, trees, foundation, plantings, rocks, and all other fixed features. The results may not be perfect, but they will give you a good idea of the effects of different color combinations.

Certain general house styles have been popular over time and throughout the United States. Almost all older towns and cities have examples of Colonials, Victorians, Italianate houses, bungalows, and ranches.

White is still America's favorite exterior paint color. It has been used for hundreds of years. This preference began during the Greek Revival era of 1825-1855. For years, historians mistakenly believed that ancient Greek buildings were painted in pale and muted colors. In fact, all important ancient buildings were actually painted in bright, rich greens, blues, reds, and yellows. Brilliant colors were used on buildings throughout the world.

Colonial

From the mid-1600s to about 1780, European immigrants to the New World brought along their building and color styles that would become known as Colonials. They had a limited range of pigments from which to choose. The homes usually had one or two stories and were boxlike. They were built two rooms deep and had symmetrical windows. The first Colonial homes were built mostly along the East Coast, the Gulf Coast, and in parts of the Southwest. Typical exterior colors were shades of red, orange, ocher, blue, green, gray, and brown.

Federal

From about 1780 to 1830, the Federal style dominated American architecture. Most original Federal-style homes are located on the East Coast and in portions of the South, such as Georgia and South Carolina. The Federal style is characterized by its symmetry and delicacy. Homes are usually boxlike and rectangular. They may have an elliptical fanlight over the front door and sidelights on either side of the door. There may be columns, pilasters, and curved or octagonal sections. Federal houses usually have windows recessed into arches and curving steps. Because more paint colors was available, houses were painted in a wider range of the tints and shades of existing colors, such as peach and bright green.

Greek Revival

In their first 40 years of independence, Americans gave up complex European house styles, replacing them with simple, stately homes. The Greek Revival style was first seen in Philadelphia's public buildings. Between 1825 and 1855, it became popular in the rural Northeast and the Midwest and predominated in urban houses of those regions well into the twentieth century. The form is that of a classical temple, with a front gable and portico. The front door is usually flanked by narrow sidelights and features a row of transom lights above. Wide pilasters, deep, heavy cornices, and Greek ornaments, such as the Greek fret, are characteristic. The full-colonnaded Greek mansion in Southern states became an icon in American architecture. Greek Revivals were almost always painted white.

Gothic and Italianate Revival

Between 1840 and 1900, architectural reformers offered three main new styles in place of Greek Revival designs: Gothic, Italianate, and Victorian.

Gothic

The Gothic style is characterized by the upward direction of the leading lines—vertical, steep-pitched roofs, board-and-batten siding, and sharply pointed dormers, gables, and ornamentation.

Italianate

This style was derived from the Italian villa or farmhouse and features a characteristic square tower or cupola. It has a low-pitched roof with an overhang supported by brackets. It usually has a broad veranda or porch and a flat-roofed tower. Windows are characteristically rounded.

Victorian

Victorian house styles are those popular during the reign of Britain's Queen Victoria, comprising much of the nineteenth century. With them came the concept that homes and their colors should be in harmony with nature.

Victorian houses are generally divided into two classifications: early and late. They incorporated complex shapes and ornate detailing. Characteristic of these homes are an asymmetrical facade, multicolored walls, and steeply pitched roofs, often featuring cross gables, patterned shingles, conical turrets, dormers, and decorative brackets beneath the eaves. Finials and cresting decorate roof ridges. In earlier Victorians, the mansard roof is the most distinctive feature. House color in the later Victorians included darker body colors in browns, olives, reds, and oranges. Often, these later homes had color schemes in which one color was painted on the upper body of the house and another on the lower.

Bungalow

Rustic bungalows and modest Colonials took the place of Victorians between about 1890 and 1940. By 1910, the bungalow emerged as the all-American family house. Its popularity spread from the West Coast to the East, the opposite of all previous housing fads, and the craze went on through the 1930s. The bungalow is built of natural materials such as fieldstone, cobblestone, board and batten, stucco, shingles, or clapboard. It is, ideally, a one-story structure with a wide, low-pitched roof and a front porch. The bungalow is economical, simple, and functional. Most built in the early twentieth century were painted with the same deep, rich colors as the Victorians. However, some were painted with a medium body color and white trim or a medium body color and dark trim.

Colonial Revival

The Colonial Revival became one of the dominant home styles throughout the United States during the first half of the twentieth century. Colonial Revivals were free interpretations of historical Colonials. The house has a balanced facade. Windows are symmetrically balanced with double-hung sashes. Front doors are usually surrounded with sidelights, fanlights, crown moldings, and pediments. The front entrance may be accentuated with columns or a portico. The roof may be gambrel style, center-gabled, side-gabled, or hipped. Victorian colors were replaced with primary colors, monochromatic tones, and white. Color became the enemy of form. Designers felt it detracted from the shape of the house.

Ranch House

By 1945, in postwar America, the return of 13 million service men and women created a massive housing shortage. 3,600,000 families were without homes. Ranch houses provided the solution.

Architect Cliff May created the first ranch house design in the early 1930's. He favored a Spanish Colonial style. All ranch house styles were economical to build, simple in design, informal, one-story structures, with low pitched eaves, picture windows and a rambling plan. They were enthusiastically promoted in magazines.

The ranch and its successor, the split-level, are still popular in wide ranges of color.

Note: This book does not address authentic historical color use appropriate to the date, type, and style of any building at the time of its design and construction. For this information, or for a qualified historically and scientifically trained consultant, or for information on historical preservation or restoration, call the State Historic Preservation Office, National Trust for Historic Preservation, 1785 Massachusetts Avenue, Washington, D.C. 20036, or a regional office of the National Park Service.

Resources

Paint Manufacturers

Use these phone numbers and/or Web sites to locate dealers in your area, and find answers to specific questions about manufacturers' products. Unless otherwise noted, companies listed offer multiple product lines of oil- and water-based paints; most also manufacture glazes, primers, and other products for interior painting.

Ace

www.acehardware.com/paintbrand/
paintbrand.asp

Behr

3400 W. Segerstrom Avenue
Santa Ana, CA 92704

1-800-854-0133 (extension 3 for store locations; extension 2 for technical questions)

www.behrpaint.com

Benjamin Moore

51 Chestnut Ridge Road
Montvale, NJ 07645
1-88-BENMOORE

For your closest Benjamin Moore dealer please call 1-8006PAINT6 (1-800-672-4686) or visit their Web site at www.benjaminmoore.com. Benjamin Moore is a registered trademark and Color Preview is a trademark of Benjamin Moore & Co.

California Paints

1-617-547-5300

Crayola Paints

This is a line of paints manufactured by Benjamin Moore. In addition to a range of Crayola colors, such specialty products as glitter paint, chalkboard paint, and glow-in-the-dark paint are available for special painted effects. For more information, call the Benjamin Moore customer service number (1-888-BENMOORE) or access the company's Web site and search by the brand name.

Devoe

1-800-654-2616
www.devoepaint.com

Dutch Boy

1-800-828-5669
www.dutchboy.com

Finnaren & Haley Paint Company

This is a regional company with retail outlets in Pennsylvania, New Jersey, and Delaware.

Conshohocken, PA
1-800-843-9800
www.fhpaint.com

Glidden

1-800-221-4100
www.gliddenpaint.com

Pittsburgh Paints

1-800-441-9695
www.pittsburghpaints.com

Pratt & Lambert

1-800-289-7728
www.prattandlambert.com

Sherwin-Williams

1-800-4-SHERWIN
www.sherwin-williams.com

Super Premium Paint Brands

The following group of paint companies is distinguished by their high-quality, premium priced products. The approach to color of these brands is quite complex; each paint color is composed of multiple pigments (up to a dozen, sometimes more); pigment is the most expensive component in paint, and thus theses paints have a retail cost of more than double that of other high-quality paints. However, in addition to the complexity of their color system, these paints also provide a wall finish that is distinctive for its depth and luminosity of color.

Farrow & Ball

British Manufacturer. Mail of online order paints (oil enamels cannot be shipped to Arizona or California). Sample pots available; manufacturer recommends customers send for product literature and/or samples before making a quantity order.

Phone (in Toronto, Canada) 1-845-369-4912 (limited distribution at select U.S. outlets)
www.farrow-ball.com

Fine Paints of Europe

Exclusive importer of Holland-made Schreuder Paints. Fine Paints offers many high-quality products for preparation, plus best-quality paintbrushes and other equipment. In addition to its line of 940 fan deck colors and Classic European colors, Fine Paints also offers Martha's Fine Paints, a collection of nearly 100 colors developed in collaboration with Martha Stewart Living Omnimedia, Inc.

Sample .25 liter pots are available for 99 colors of the company's Obolux ä matte acrylic paints. Distributed nationwide through select local dealers, and by mail order.

P.O. Box 419
Route 4 West
Woodstock, VT 05091
1-800-332-1556
www.finepaints.com

Donald Kaufman Color Collection

Another producer of premium, full-spectrum color paints; these are available through two retail outlets, one in New Jersey and the other in Santa Monica, California. For information, call 1-800-977-9198

Ecofriendly Paint Production

Many of the paint manufacturers listed above have low- or no-VOC paint lines; the following companies make only low- or no-VOC products. Many are produced with alternative ingredients with low or very little toxicity. For specific information about the products, contact the manufacturers at the phone numbers and or Web sites listed.

American Formulating & Manufacturing (AFM)

350 W. Ash Street, #700
San Diego, CA 92101
1-800-239-0321
(leave name to receive product brochure)

1-619-239-0321 (for technical information)

Safecoat products: primers, paints, clear finishes, sealants

www.afmsafecoat.com

Bioshield Paint Co.

1365 Rufina Circle
Santa Fe, NM 87505
1-800-621-2591 (orders, catalogs)
1-505-438-3448 (questions, comments)

Casein (milk) paint, color washes, organic color pigments, gloss and satin enamel paint, plus a wide assortment of paintbrushes, specialty finish brushes, and painting combs.

www.bioshieldpaint.com

Chem-Safe Products Company

P.O Box 33023
San Antonio, TX 78265
1-210-657-5321

Enviro-Safe Paints (available in flat, satin, and semigloss)

Innovative Formulations Corporation

1810 S. 6th Avenue
Tucson, AZ 85713
1-800-346-7265

Ecological and Canary lines of paint have no known carcinogens or neurotoxins (available in flat, eggshell, semigloss, and gloss).

Miller Paint Co. Inc.

317 S.E. Grand Avenue
Portland, OR 97214
1-503-233-4491

Miller Low Biocide Paint (available in flat,
satin, and semigloss). Solvent-free, low-biocide,
low-fungicide paints.

Murco Wall Products

300 N.E. 21st Street
Fort Worth, TX 76106
1-800-446-7214

Auro Natural Paints

Made in Germany and packaged as a powder,
made exclusively from natural sources.

The Old-Fashioned Milk Paint Company

For over 25 years this company has manufactured and distributed genuine milk paints. The
product is sold at retail stores around the U.S.
(call or check Web site for dealers), or by direct
mail order.

436 Main Street
P.O. Box 222
Groton, MA 01450
1-978-448-2754
www.milkpaint.com

More Information about Paint

Questions about the ingredients of a high-quality
paint? The Paint Quality Institute provides the
facts, plus loads of professional pointers on getting the best result for your painting labors. The
Institute's Web site has lots of answers. Visit at
www.paintquality.com

The National Paint and Coatings Association
(NPCA) offers a Web site providing extensive
information about paints, painting, and choosing
paint colors. The site also provides easy links to
many commercial how-to Web pages. Visit at
www.paintinfo.org

Want to do the research, then hire a pro? The
Paint and Decorating Contractors of America
(PDCA) is a 115-year-old professional organiza-
tion to which 3,100 painting companies belong.
Their Web site provides helpful hints about hiring a pro, plus a convenient 800 number to find
local, trained, and licensed painting contractors
in your area. Visit the PDCA Web site at
www.pdca.org and click on "consumer information."

Learn about Lead

Homes built before 1978 may have existing paint
that contains lead as its hiding agent. Before dis-
turbing a surface that may possibly contain this
toxin, learn the facts. The U.S. Environmental
Protection Agency staffs a lead hotline and offers
information on its Web site about detecting, abat-
ing, and/or eliminating a lead paint problem in
the home. Hotline staffers will send on request a
comprehensive packet of informational brochures
(which are also downloadable from the Web site).
Contact them before painting. The NPCA consumer Web site described above
(www.paintinfo.org) also offers links to comprehensive information about lead paint. EPA Web
site: www.epa.gov/lead

National Lead Information Center

1-800-242-5323

More Color Advice

Which colors are hot this year? And which colors
are emerging as the trendsetters in home furnishings? The Color Marketing Group's member-
ship is composed of 1,700 Color Designers whose
task is to "interpret, create, forecast, and select"
colors for all kinds of commercial goods and
businesses. Check out their Web site at www.col-
ormarketing.org; click on "site-at-a-glance" and
then "news releases" to get the latest word on
fashionable colors.

The color wheel is a very logical way to approach
color selection; a well-constructed wheel can provide instant information on harmonious combinations of the primary, secondary, and tertiary
hues. The Color Wheel Company produces a
series of color wheels for artists, designers,
and consumers to help them construct pleasing
palettes based on the relationship of spectral
colors on the wheel. The 9 1/4" color wheel and
Interior Design wheel provide lots of information
about color, and are reasonably priced. For product listings and prices, contact:

The Color Wheel Company

P.O. Box 130
Philomath, OR 97370-0130
1-541-929-7526
www.colorwheelco.com

While most large home stores and specialty paint
stores offer good selections of painting tools and
equipment, the following offer helpful information or specialty supplies on their Web sites.

Gregor Cann

Cann Design
1-760-318-7925 (West Coast)
1-617-293-6078 (East Coast)
canndesign@aol.com

Tools

The Wooster Brush Company
Wooster, OH 44691
1-800-392-7246 (customer service)
www.woosterbrush.com

Manufacturers of more than 2,000 different painting products, including brushes, rollers, and other tools. The Web site has painting tips and offers a good overview of innovative products for painting.

Special-Effects Supplies

McCloskey Special Effects

(a division of the Vaispar Corporation)
Wheeling, IL 60090
1-800-345-4530 (product information)

McCloskey makes a variety of glazing products for broken color effects, and the company offers a number of helpful brochures along with their products that supply tips and hints for successful finishes.

Faux Like a Pro

P.O. Box 1420
Brookline, MA 02446
1-617-713-4320
www.fauxlikeapro.com

This company's comprehensive Web site offers technique advice, a live chat room, and an online store for ordering paints, tools, and books. Designed for professional faux-finishers, the Web site is also a great learning tool and source for interested amateur painters. The company has its own line of special-effects paints.

American Home Stencils

10007 S. 76th Street
Franklin, WI 53132
1-800-742-4520 (M-F, 8-4 CST)
www.americanhomestencils.com

Order stencils and supplies online or request a catalog. This company offers Robert Simmons stencil brushes, reasonably prices products recommended by the decorative painters used in chapter three of Painting Inside & Out.

Adele Bishop Stencils

P.O. Box 477
Campbellville, Ontario, L0P 1B0
Canada
www.adelebishop.com
Fax: 1-905-854-1243

Large selections of stencils and stenciling supplies. Catalog $4 U.S. Place orders by mail. No credit cards.

L.A. Stencilworks

16115 Vanowen Street
Van Nuys, CA 91406
1-877-989-0262
www.lastencil.com

Large selections of stencils, including many contemporary designs. Multiple designs can be used together to create interesting decorative murals.

Decorative Painters

Find these through designers and home decorators near you.

Bonnie's Place

27 Westchester Avenue
Pound Ridge, NY 10576
1-914-764-8699

Photo Credits

Abode, 74; 80 (top); 86; 94 (right); 111; 113

Sandy Agrafiotis, 5; 77; 173 (top); 230

Fernando Bengoechea/Franca Speranza srl, 64; 80 (bottom); 84

Antoine Bootz, 3; 62; 76; 78; 79; 89; 101

Grey Crawford, 73; 87

Courtesy of the Glidden Company, 43-47; 155-163; 190; 282; 283

Sam Gray, 173 (second from bottom); 175 (top & middle); 194; 195; 213; 220; 223; 271

Peter Gridley/FPG International, 2 (bottom); 218

Steve Gross & Susan Daley, 61

John Hall, 110

Brian Harrison/Elizabeth Whiting & Associates, 71; 105

Douglas Keister, 2 (top); 173 (bottom); 174 (second from top); 197; 201; 206; 207; 208; 216, 217; 228; 232; 233; 239; 243; 255; 261; 262; 266; 267; 267; 277; 280; 281 (bottom)

Keller & Keller, 62

Tom Leighton/Elizabeth Whiting & Associates, 96

Keith Scott Morton, 83; 93

Peter Paige/Antine Shin LLC, 67

Spike Powell/Elizabeth Whiting & Associates, 70; 103

Greg Premru, 58

Picture Press, Deco, Photographer: Nüttgens, 148

Eric Roth, 1 (top); 65; 72; 88; 90; 92; 97; 104; 106; 174 (middle); 175 (bottom); 234; 246; 251; 252; 281 (top)

Eric Roth/Cann Design, 100; 115-119

Eric Roth/Astrid Vigeland Design, 109

Report Bilder-Dienst, Freundin, Manduzio, 146 (left)

Report Bilder-Dienst, Freundin, Spachmann, 147 (right)

Report Bilder-Dienst, © U2 Fotodesign, 146 (right); 147 (left)

James R. Salomon, 202; 258; 272

The Society for The Preservation of New England Antiquities, 211; 265

Brian Vanden Brink, 174 (top, second from bottom, & bottom); 192; 199; 205; 225; 227; 237; 241; 248; 269; 275

Brian Vanden Brink/Rick Burt, Architect, 256

Brian Vanden Brink/Warren Hall, Architect, 277

Brian Vanden Brink/Mark Hutker Architects, 257

Brain Vanden Brink/Quinn Evans, Architect, 244

Brian Vanden Brink/Stephen Foote, Architect, 60

Brian Vanden Brink/James Sterling, Architect, 245

Steve Vierra/Gayle Reynolds Design, 102

Andreas von Einsiedel/Red Cover, 63

David Wakely/Cathy Schwabe/EHDD Architecture, © 2001, 215

Henry Wilson/The Interior Archive, 94 (left); 99

Studio Photography by Bobbie Bush and Kevin Thomas

About the Authors

Judy Ostrow is an independent journalist who specializes in writing about the home, its architecture, interior design, and renovation. Her articles have appeared in many national magazines, including Home, Natural Home, This Old House, and special publications of House Beautiful and Woman's Day. She has painted many rooms of the home she shares with her husband and two children in Westchester County, New York, and is currently planning the painted interior of the family's vacation house in Stonington, Maine.

Virginia Patterson is a fine arts–trained painter. For more than ten years, she has been commissioned to paint everything from traditional canvases to decorative indoor and outdoor murals to unusual objects such as mailboxes, flower boxes, glass pieces, and more. Ms. Patterson regularly restores furniture for interior designers, including staining and upholstery, and has also designed and painted furniture pieces in her original designs. Additionally, Virginia is an accomplished quilter whose work has been exhibited in galleries and art shows across the United States.

Francine Hornberger has been an editor of interior design and crafts books for many years. In that time, she's written for and worked with several accomplished crafters and large-name crafts products manufacturers and crafts books publishers, including the Offray Ribbon Company and McCall's Creates.

Bonnie Rosser Krims is the author of The Perfect Palette (Warner Books) and one of a handful of nationally recognized professional paint-color consultants in the United States. She is also an accomplished painter whose work has been widely exhibited, most notably as part the Andy Warhol/Frank Stella show at the Morgan Gallery in Boston.

Bonnie's consulting business is based in Massachusetts, but she consults with clients throughout the country via the Web and the U.S. mail. You can contact her through her Web site, theperfectpalette.com, or at The Emerson Umbrella Center for the Arts, 40 Stow Street in Concord, Massachusetts, 01742.